The TRUTH® is a registered trademark of Primos, Inc.
dba Primos Hunting Calls and is used
by Ronnie "Cuz" Strickland and
Stoeger Publishing Company with permission and license.

Published by Stoeger Publishing Company
17603 Indian Head Highway, Suite 200
Accokeek, Maryland 20607
www.stoegerindustries.com

Library of Congress Catalog Card No: 2002110082

BK0220
ISBN: 0-88317-260-7

Printed in Korea

Distributed to the book trade and to the sporting goods trade by
Stoeger Industries
17603 Indian Head Highway, Suite 200
Accokeek, Maryland 20607
Tel: 301-283-6300 Fax: 301-263-6986

Edited by: Kevin Tate
Publishing Assistant: Terry Mullen
Jacket Design: Art Shirley
Cover Photograph: Paul T. Brown
Hard-Cover Turkey Photographic Image: Paul T. Brown

THE TRUTH®
About Spring Turkey Hunting
According to Cuz

Ronnie "Cuz" Strickland

Stoeger Publishing
Great Outdoor Books Since 1925

NATIONAL WILD TURKEY FEDERATION

Of all the successful wildlife restoration stories in this country, the come-back of the wild turkey may be the most outstanding. From the brink of extinction, the wild turkey is now a common sight in most of the United States and parts of Canada and Mexico. This turn around has been the result of thousands of people focused on one goal, protecting and sustaining this nation's most spectacular game bird.

The National Wild Turkey Federation has been paramount in this effort and is working harder than ever for the wild turkey. When the NWTF was founded in 1973, there were only 1.3 million turkeys throughout the United States. Since then, that number has more than tripled and now stands at 4.8 million birds thanks to the NWTF, its members, partners, and state wildlife agencies.

Together the NWTF's conservation partners and grassroots members have raised and spent more than $90 million on projects benefiting wild turkeys throughout the United States, Mexico, and Canada. As rich as these triumphs have been in raising funds to enhance wild turkey populations, there is still much work to do. With a growing force of member volunteers and dedicated partners, there is no limit to what can be accomplished.

I am proud to be a member of the NWTF. To find out how you can join and help the wild turkey call 1-800-THE-NWTF.

TABLE OF CONTENTS

What can I say about "The Cuz"? The best huntin' buddy a man can have. And a more dedicated business partner than anyone deserves. Without a doubt he's the most delightful, creative storyteller, writer, and character you'll ever be around. Yeah, all of the above and most of all my blood brother for life!

I just hope the hunting world realizes just how enormous his contribution to the success of Mossy Oak has been. Simply immeasurable.

If one thing is for certain, it's that his most entertaining talent is the "true stories" he always tells. I couldn't possibly count the times he has captivated a "Mossy Oak" audience, whether one or one hundred, and brought the house down with his tales-all of which he insist are true stories-hence The Truth becomes a perfect name for his stories.

I've often longed to figure out a way to share with the rest of the outdoor world the laughter, fun, mischief, and great times, not to mention love of fellow and wildlife that make up the very special persona of "The Cuz". This book and its tales offer a great sample of such.

Toxey Haas

When I first met Cuz, I was trying to sell him some turkey calls for the Sporting Goods store where he worked in Natchez, Mississippi. That was 1986, and little did I know how he would impact my life.

We immediately started talking about turkeys and Cuz asked me if I wanted to see some video footage he and his turkey hunting buddies had shot. I wanted to produce a turkey hunting video as a sequel to my first instructional tape, so needless to say I was interested. Some of Cuz's footage was shaky, but it was real, and that's how we got together.

I hired Cuz to gather video footage for the first Primos hunting tape and at the end of 1987 spring season, Cuz and I sat down to look at what we had. Cuz had gathered plenty of footage and we needed a name for the video. Cuz said, "Well, some of it is still a little shaky." I replied, "But it's the truth!" I knew right then that was the name we were looking for. With no more discussion, we headed to the edit room and The TRUTH, video series was born.

That first turkey hunting, video was a huge success and through the years thousands of turkey hunters have come to know Cuz. I can't think of a name that ever fit anybody any better. Cuz is someone who will always make you laugh, whether in person or in this book. He just has a special way of telling his experiences that will make you slap your knee.

Cuz is your "Cuz," too. Or "cousin," as the Northerners might say. Reading this book won't replace being with Cuz in camp watching him fix biscuits and gravy, telling jokes and making folks laugh but it's the next best thing.

Enjoy!

Will Primos

Introduction

I have been blessed in my life with many gifts. A wonderful wife, two great daughters, parents who taught me right from wrong, friends who would make any man proud. I have been able to spend thousands of hours in the field and call it work. I have been able to watch my girls hunt, hit a home run and dance a ballet. I have been able to travel and hunt in other countries. I have shared camps with men who were true legends in the outdoors. I have heard elk bugle, seen caribou migrate, watched turkeys strut, whitetails fight, moose feed and ducks cup and commit. To say that my time on this earth has been precious would be a fair statement.

Much of my time in the field has been with a video camera in tow. I have seen hundreds of hunts unfold and watched thousands of animals through a one inch black-and-white viewfinder. Some people think I have missed my hunting prime by carrying a camera in the field. No one walking the earth enjoys the sights, sounds, smells and emotions of the hunt more than I, and I still hunt with gun and bow often, and I still get shaky knees when a buck approaches into bow range or a strutting gobbler appears. As much as I love the hunt, I love to share it even more. Carrying a video camera afield for almost two decades has allowed me the privilege of sharing with millions of people some wonderful moments that would have otherwise been only a brief chat around a campfire.

Nothing in this book will help balance the budget, establish world peace or have any effect on the stock market. It may, however, give you a few hours of entertainment, answer some questions about turkey hunting's challenges and, hopefully, bring a smile to your face.

Cuz

THE TRUTH®

About Spring Turkey Hunting
According to Cuz

———————◆———————

Ronnie "Cuz" Strickland

The "If Onlys"

Over the years I've heard thousands of "if onlys" from turkey hunters. If only that gobbler had come another three steps. If only I could hunt that property across the creek. If only I had not called that last time.

For me, it's special each and every time I get into the woods. Some people have life changing experiences that make them appreciate things like spring mornings more than others. I have had several of these experiences that have kept my perspectives clear. The only "if only" I have ever mentioned during turkey season is "if only" there weren't any snakes.

Will Primos once told me that turkey hunting was like a cult. If that's true, then there are a couple of million other turkey hunters who are aware that I am deathly afraid of snakes. I don't mean walk-away-and-make-a-face-when-you-see-one scared, I mean can't-even-watch-those-shows-on-the-Discovery-Channel scared.

I'm not sure when this phobia kicked in but I feel it was later in life. I can remember fishing with my dad and having many snake encounters of one type or another. It seemed the more close calls I had, the worse things became. The problem here is once you've established yourself as a bonified snake hater, then every jerk in the woods wants to throw one on you.

Here's a warning, kind of like those labels on non-prescription drugs. If you run into me turkey hunting, fishing, playing golf or at the mall, don't throw a live, dead or rubber snake on me. You could get hurt.

That's not a threat or some macho defensive response, it's just that my reaction to snakes is usually violent. You may be standing in the path I need to take to get clear. That could be dangerous.

My good friend Bubba found this out the hard way one spring morning in the Homochitto National Forest. We struck a turkey near what we called the low water bridge. There was a dry sandy creek bed nearby that made slipping in close to the turkey a breeze. Once we thought we were even with the last gobble, we decided to climb the creek bank and ease into the woods. I went first with Bubba behind me. The creek bank was steep and Bubba was in a hurry, so he grabbed my boot to give me a boost. When my head and, more importantly, my eyes were even with the top, I was eye to eye with a very full-grown snake. To this day I can't tell you what type it was. They all look alike to me. When I momentarily froze at the top of the bank, Bubba decided I needed more boost from his end. Big mistake on his part.

Not only did I avoid the snake in record time, I kicked Bubba so far back that he hit the bank on the opposite side of the creek, which made the turkey gobble once again. Bubba now walks in front whenever we're hunting together.

Close encounters with serpents are almost a regular occurrence with me. I'm pretty sure I see so many snakes because I look for them. That's why I don't squirrel hunt: Too much looking up and not enough looking down.

Sometimes looking down isn't enough. One of my more violent reactions took place in south Texas. I was following a hunter with my video camera on my shoulder.

He was in the middle of a world-class sneak and I was determined to stay with him and get the hunt on tape. I was watching his every step and putting my boots into his tracks. We only needed a few more yards before sitting down and setting up.

With only a few steps left, I caught movement to my right. A huge blue indigo snake was making a beeline for my feet. If you've never seen a blue indigo snake in Texas, let me tell you, they can grow to giant proportions. This one must have been seven or eight feet long and as big around as my arm. I'm sure the snake wasn't coming at me, but at the time it certainly appeared to be.

I made a lighting fast move to my left to prepare to jump and run. When I did, I raked across a thorn that looked like a tigers tooth on a fly rod. This thorn slashed through my shirt just above my belt and opened me up like an over-ripe melon. When the hunter looked back to see the source of all the commotion the snake was gone and I was bleeding from my belt to my boots. When I told him what had happened, he smiled and reminded me that blue indigo snakes won't bite and, if they did, they weren't poisonous. He might have thought differently had my escape path taken me up his back instead of into the tiger tooth thorn tree.

As I stated earlier, once you get the reputation of being scared of snakes, then every macho man in camo wants to set you up to see the spring loaded, screaming reaction that may occur. As you can imagine, I have had many of these "lets scare the crap out of Cuz" encounters.

These days, my old friends don't even try to scare me with belts, garden hoses or fan belts. First off, I've learned to be extra cautious around these guys and second, I think they've seen me jump so many times it's not as funny any more. There was a day when my old buddies planned, talked about and schemed of nothing else but how to set me into orbit. One of their classics took place on a trip to Colorado.

We were experiencing the west for the first time and were on a poor boy's budget. We drove the 1,200 miles in a van and were going to camp out. I remember saving for weeks to buy a very expensive sleeping bag. I was determined to sleep well, even if I had skimped on other items like good binoculars and boots. The first night while I was fast asleep, my buddies opened a pack of hot dog wieners and placed them strategically in my sleeping bag. The next morning when I was in the process of waking up, my leg hit one of those raw wieners and my foot touched another. By the time I was upright, which took about one second, my new expensive sleeping bag looked like an apron around my neck. I ended up using duct tape to replace the broken zippers which, in the long run, worked better as a security system.

One of the most memorable snake instances took place on another organized hunt where there were many people in camp. The hunters sharing my small cabin received a speech on opening day from yours truly about snakes, snake stories, snake tricks and the like, so I was pretty comfortable with them. On day three of the hunt one of the invited guests had an encounter with a rattlesnake. During the ride back to camp with the deceased snake in the back of the truck, one of the guides mentioned that ol' Cuz was scared of snakes.

Back at camp I was in my small cabin minding my own business, about to get the best of a homemade cheeseburger. I was sitting in a chair with a small table to my left. The guest with snake in hand slipped up and, while I was working on my burger, placed the snake on the table next to my drink. When I reached down to get a drink naturally I freaked out. What took place next is a bit of legend with the people who witnessed the event.

When I saw the snake, I jumped from the chair with plate in hand, cleared two single beds, landed across the room, missing a low hung ceiling fan, and never spilled my plate. The burger and chips were still intact, on the plate and in my right hand. I would love to see any world-class athlete even come close to pulling off that maneuver.

Needless to say, I gave the culprit a piece of my mind, but with all the laughing going on, I think my message was lost in the commotion.

I could literally write an entire book on close calls with snakes, but I can't leave the topic without sharing the most horrifying tale of all times. This encounter did not take place in some snake infested swamp or some sandy dry creek bed. It's location makes it more terrifying than if it had taken place is some area where at least you'd be on the look- out. This encounter took place in the sanctity of my own home.

I had come in late in the afternoon and, after a quick shower, had basically collapsed on the den floor. I had left a pile of gear including gun cases, duffle bags and such lying on the floor next to the front door. At some point, I was awakened by a cold chill that ran down my back. For some reason, this chill felt like a snake had brushed against my back. I told myself it was just another snake dream and closed my eyes.

When I rolled over to change positions, I caught what looked like a tail going around the hearth of the fireplace. By this time, I was wide-awake and had realized that something was really wrong.

I stood up and slowly peaked around the brick hearth and, sure enough, a snake was coiled directly under my gun cabinet. You can't imagine the shear terror that was about to take over my body.

I knew I had to dispose of the snake, but he was blocking the path to my gun cabinet. And yes I would have shot him inside my house. I called for my wife to come down and bring me something to kill a snake with. She was in the bathtub and not exactly dressed to run outside for a shovel.

I then had to make a major decision. If I run outside to get a shovel and the snake gets away, then I've got to sell my house. I opted to stay put and watch the snake. This was the longest few minutes of my life.

Finally Pam walks in and gets the picture. She returns with a shovel and I make my plan. I put one foot in a chair and the other up on the ledge of the gun cabinet. When I made my first swing with the shovel, the chair slid and I did a rather wide split. Now, I'm not built to split, so it felt like something ripped in my lower extremities. I regrouped and the second swing found its mark. So did the third, fourth, fifth and so on. Once I had taken the snake pieces outside and calmed down a bit, I noticed a swelling in my right knee. Two days later I'm in the hospital having knee surgery. I guess the snake got his licks in as well.

Looking back, I am convinced the snake had crawled into some of the gear while it was outdoors and just eased out as things calmed down. At least, I convinced myself of that so I wouldn't have to sell the house.

It all started here. This is the first gobbler Will Primos, standing, took in front of my camera. The hunt is featured on Primos' first Truth series video.

The Truth behind the Truth

To this day, one of my most vivid memories about turkey hunting came in the form of an audiotape that Will Primos produced back in the early 80s.

This small tape that, by today's standards would be trivial, had a real impact on me. It contained a few minutes of Will Primos and one of his friends, the late Russell Davis, talking about what was special about hunting wild turkeys. This tape also contained an audio recording of an actual hunt.

Will took an audio engineer into the woods, camouflaged him and recorded a successful hunt. The tape had the first redbird of the morning waking the woods, gobbling from the trees, subtle calling. It had some of Will's aggressive calling, close up gobbling and ended with a shotgun blast followed by flopping wing beats in the leaves.

Back before videotapes, this audio recording was about the coolest thing I had ever experienced. I played it over and over until I could recite each whisper and natural sound. The thought of someone taking the time to do that was amazing to me. I immediately became a Will Primos fan. It would have been hard for me to believe that a couple years later I would be working for him and attempting to do the same thing with a video camera.

Long before I met Wilbur, I talked to him on the phone a few times. I was working in a sporting goods store and buying some of his calls for resale. I used to call him and tell him how well those calls worked each time one of my customers came by with a success story. This was about the time the first consumer grade camcorders hit the market. The first one of those I saw belonged to my buddy Gary Porter.

He had purchased the camera I think for his wife to record the normal sort of family stuff. We immediately covered it in camo tape and hit the woods. We became pretty good at taping hunts and soon I was sending the footage to Will so he could see first hand how well his handmade calls were working.

One day while working behind the counter of the sporting goods store, in walks Wilbur with a camera that looked like it weighed 100 pounds. Long story short, he asked me to give this broadcast camera a try and see if we could tape a successful hunt with real camera gear. It took a while, but I learned the ins and outs of the camera and was soon a Primos employee and full time videographer. The first time I heard the term videographer I wasn't sure what it meant. I learned later that videographer is a French word meaning hernia.

In the spring of 1986 we set out to make a turkey hunting video. Unsure of what to do or how to do it, Will said, "Let's just hunt hard and we'll focus on the end result later."

The first thing we did was call Toxey Haas, who was at the time starting a small camouflage company. He called his new camouflage pattern Mossy Oak. The first time I saw Mossy Oak I knew it was tailor made for turkey hunters. We covered everything in Mossy Oak Bottomland, including cameras, decks, microphones, guns and hunters. This allowed us to move more and set up quickly. Being able to just sit down anywhere is a huge advantage when filming a turkey hunt. With Toxey's new pattern and Will's enthusiasm and still no game plan, we were ready to go.

We started around Natchez on Glasscock Island. On opening day, we were set up on a gobbling turkey and ready to make a movie.

Will called the gobbler in and to say it put on a show is an understatement. This gobbler actually hopped up on a fallen tree and strutted down the log for several feet. He hopped down and walked straight down Will's gun barrel. Our pre-planned signal for Will to shoot was a kee-kee or whistle from me. I gave the signal and Will did his part. Turkey hunt number one was in the can. The thought of being a full time wildlife videographer was pretty cool. That feeling was short lived however, when we discovered that I had not hit the record button and had simply watched the hunt through the tiny black and white viewfinder on standby.

From big time moviemaker to goat all in one fail swoop. After that miscue, we went back and got it right on the next hunt. A perfect over-the-shoulder hunt that even captured the shot wad hitting the gobbler. From that point on, we were off and rolling.

Back in those days, Will was running both the call business and a restaurant, so his time in the field was limited. I would hunt everyday with the camera and a different hunter. Will would meet me when his schedule allowed.

Along with no name and certainly no script for this video project, we also didn't have any plush locations lined up. We hunted areas close to home that we knew had turkeys. We enlisted the help of many friends who were willing to help us with the project. We hunted public land, friends' farms, hunting clubs and anywhere else we could get anywhere near a gobbling turkey.

One day while sitting at home waiting for a thunderstorm to pass, my phone rang. It was 11-year-old Will Rives.

The Rives's lived a few miles out of Natchez and were good friends who also loved the outdoors. Will's voice was shaking when I answered the phone.

"Mr. Ronnie, I've got a turkey gobbling his head off down here. Can you come help me call him up?"

Thirty minutes later Will, his dad Bill and I were standing over an old gobbler and I had one of the best hunts of the season in the can. It was clear that when we thought we would never get enough footage, we would receive a gift from above.

During the season we learned the video footage was much more exciting if you could get the turkeys to gobble, strut, or both. In order to do this, more excited calling was the key. We would cutt and cackle much more than was needed just to get the gobbler into gun range. This is certainly where the "calling too much and too loud" handle was stuck on Wilbur and me. To this day, I hear from turkey hunters about the calling too much and too loud thing. I can only imagine how many times Will has had to address that issue.

One of our favorite calls used for locating gobblers after fly down was a combination of Will's excited yelps and me cutting on a tube call. Will dubbed that the "Rodney Shuffle." I know that old time turkey hunters would just cringe at the thought of all the calling, but it seemed to be the thing to do. It certainly provoked more exciting responses from some gobblers. I'm sure it probably scared a few of them too.

The bottom line is, even with all the added weight of the camera gear and the pressure of having to find turkeys, it was still fun.

Back then, there were no guidelines, no edit decisions, no lux factors or filter choices to make. It was all about hunting and hoping the footage turned out.

For 44 straight days I carried that camera and hunted pretty much all day long. Looking back, the one person I can say without a doubt that helped make the video happen from my end was my wife Pam. During those early days, she had to not only run the house but also help with hunters and writers that were constantly guests in our home. She cooked meals for strangers who became friends. She talked turkey without knowing much about it and never complained once about being awakened at 4 a.m. by staggering camo clad strangers in the house. It was a grueling schedule and a season that I won't ever forget. We captured some great hunts that included smiles and frowns, misses and miscues and a lot of the emotion that goes along with turkey hunting.

One night while viewing some footage of a clean miss I remarked that the footage was a bit shaky. Will replied, "Yeah but it's the truth".

So came the name of the first video and the "Truth" series was born. After the edit session that educated more than one video engineer about yelps and cuts and struts, the first "Truth About Spring Turkey Hunting" was complete. The cover of the video was a group photo of some of the many people who made it possible.

Today Primos and Mossy Oak have taken hunting videos and even outdoor TV to another level. Equipment is better, techniques are better and certainly we have better plans. It's still fun for me to put that original video in and watch a little bit of history being made. It was one of the first videos, it was certainly one of the best videos, and it was, without question, the truth.

MRI

When the clock finally sounded off, I was already dressed and ready to go. No way I was going to be late for this turkey hunt.

To say I was green to the sport of turkey hunting would be fair. I had been on many turkey hunts and had received some good lessons from the gobblers. I was now ready to get a lesson from a master turkey hunter. Mr. Tom was a legend in southwest Mississippi. He had been hunting turkeys forever. The fact that he was letting me tag along made this day special. I was finally going to hear the golden call, see the magic bullet and watch the master at work.

The hunt started more slowly than I had anticipated. We met at our pre-determined location and Mr. Tom was sipping coffee and reading a newspaper. I had a million questions for Mr. Tom, but sat silent while he sipped his coffee and thumbed the paper.

"Sit down boy we've got lots of time," he said.

After what seemed like an hour he fired up his Jeep wagon and headed north. By the time we made the twenty-mile trip, dawn was already peaking through the trees. As we walked through the woods, Mr. Tom could sense my impatience and reminded me twice more during the walk we had plenty of time.

We were still walking when I heard the gobbler sound off. Soon another joined in and finally four gobblers were waking up the world from the tall pines that were still a distance away. Mr. Tom turned east away from the gobbling birds and once again he could tell I was confused.

"Calm down. We're going to where they'll end up."

Sure enough, we set up on the edge of a large pasture and one hour and 40 minutes later, the gobblers showed.

A few soft yelps were all the golden calls I heard from Mr. Tom. I shot the biggest of the gobblers at 25 yards.

"I told you we had plenty of time son. Ya' need to calm down some if you're gonna hunt these turkeys."

For the next half hour, Mr. Tom went on to explain to me what our story would be when asked. I learned that he shared these woods with two other hunters and wanted his story and mine to match when we were called on. The story he concocted took longer than the hunt. It was elaborate and detailed in every aspect. What we heard, which was only one, where we were and how the hunt went down.

Sure enough, when we returned to the Jeep, there was a camo clad stranger sitting on the ground smoking a pipe. My palms began to sweat as the hunter spoke.

"What'd you boys do this morning?"

I froze.

Mr. Tom went into our well-rehearsed story and his words and actions made it sound as if had happened just that way. The hunter never looked at Mr. Tom, only at me. I smiled and nodded my head in agreement with each spin of the tale. Finally the confrontation ended when the other hunter put out his pipe picked up his double barrel and walked away. My first lesson in MRI truly came from a master.

I learned early on that turkey hunters are a different breed. Those same people that you see in church that you help coach with in little league and that sell you insurance are living double lives. If they turkey hunt, they have a dark side. They are able to withhold information and obtain secrets with the skill of a trained CIA agent.

I have two terms I often use to describe seasoned turkey hunters. They are "politely evasive" and "conveniently absent minded." To this day I am amazed at how universal this character trait is among turkey hunters.

It makes no difference what part of the country you're in. Turkey hunters are masters at obtaining and holding MRI, or Most Recent Information. Even between best friends who have shared things since childhood, recent information on gobbling turkeys can be clouded and misleading at best. For example, I was with a fellow once on his hunting lease and from one listening location at dawn we heard seven gobblers. When the morning hunt was over and we returned to camp, he was asked by his best hunting buddy, who happened to be his brother, what we had heard. His reply was, "We heard that old gobbler down by Clear Creek sound off and one other way off."

Now there was nothing untrue about that statement. We

indeed did hear a gobbler down by Clear Creek and another way off. He simply left out the information on the other five gobblers that were choking themselves all in close proximity to our location. True enough, MRI is crucial to turkey hunting success, so it's no wonder that some hunters have taken this ability to untold levels.

I tend to stay away from labels like sneaky, slippery, shifty, devious, or tricky, but all these terms could be used according to who you're referring to or conversing with. That's not to say that being slick about obtaining information is a bad thing, it's just a part of the game. There are countless ways to obtain good MRI both before and during the season. One of the masters of this maneuver was a fellow who used to cut my hair at the barbershop in my hometown. Looking back I'm pretty sure this guy got into cutting hair just to get MRI.

He would ease his way into conversations with landowners, rural mail carriers and yes, even hunters, to get information on where a gobbling turkey may be hanging out. When talking with these people, he would make it sound as though he was a terrible hunter and needed some help. He could even make hunters feel as though they needed to lend him a helping hand. This guy could have easily been a con artist who took advantage of unsuspecting people.

He would go into great detail about how bad his calling was, how he couldn't get a break and soon, the invitations and information were flowing like a river.

In reality, this guy was a machine in the woods. His home-made handcrafted slates were world class and his hunting savvy was equally as good. The only thing this guy was better at than hunting turkeys was getting information.

Back in the days when you could gain access to land just by asking, I think he would trade his hair cutting services for turkey hunting rights. One thing for sure, he always had places to hunt and turkeys to chase.

Today some of the best information on where turkeys hang out can come from deer hunters. I have several friends who join two or three deer hunting clubs just to get MRI. They will make several camp visits during the deer season. They never deer hunt and instead, will cook elaborate meals and clean up around the camp. All the time they are gaining valuable information on turkeys that may wander by strategically placed deer stands. Like I said, turkey hunters are a different breed.

As for me, I have always had a few close friends who can rely on me to shoot them straight. In turn they did the same for me.

When your turkey hunting area is 100 percent public hunting ground, you surely would like to see your huntin' buddy rather than a stranger smack an old gobbler that you can't hunt for one reason or another. Once this confidence or agreement is broken, then it's every man or turkey hunter for himself.

When you hunt with real friends, there are other ways to pass along MRI that are not as subtle as when dealing with just other hunters. You can be more direct in your responses and generally tell the whole truth.

My good friend Bubba used to have several ways to pass along MRI when we were hunting the same area. Once in the national forest close to home, I returned to my truck around 7:30a.m. and found one gobbler breast feather stuck under my windshield wiper. Another time I found a small smearing of gobbler blood on my door handle.

The best of all personal messages from Bubba was in the form of a small note stuck to my truck window, again with a smearing of gobbler blood. I had told Bubba that I had heard two gobblers in a certain area and he should go in there and try his luck. He was having a slow season and his real job was keeping him almost too busy to hunt.

Deep down Bubba knew what I meant when I passed this particular MRI along to him. What it really meant was I had a gobbling turkey located and wanted to make sure Bubba didn't get in there before I did.

The note read, "You said I'd hear one from the brickyard plot. You said he'd be west and he's probably hot. I stopped by your truck, heard two, and moved fast. Now ones in my truck and you can kiss my ass". Bubba always had a sense of humor and could tell when I with holding information and spreading a smoke screen.

Do You Believe?

My drive to the Jackson, Mississippi airport was a bit depressing. Dark clouds gathered, the wind was picking up and the smell of rain was heavy.

When the Delta flight landed and my outdoor writer friend Joe Byers stepped off the plane, the rain started. Small drops at first, and then a steady flow. By the time we made the 90-minute drive to Greenwood, it was coming down in sheets.

I managed to get Joe's gear inside the camp where Will Primos was waiting without drowning. Will extended his hand and said, "Sorry about the weather Joe."

"No problem," was Joe's response.

I thought to myself, he's taking this pretty well. What I didn't know at the time was Joe meant it's not a problem for him to hunt turkeys in a rainstorm. When he reappeared ten minutes later in full Mossy Oak camouflage and a rain suit on his arm, Will and I both got the message.

"We ready?" was all Joe said.

Will looked at me. We both looked at Joe as he made his way to the door. There was no doubt that Joe was ready to hunt rain or no rain. To make matters even more challenging, he was carrying a black powder shotgun.

I started to weigh the odds in my mind. First, it was raining so hard you couldn't hear yourself think. Second, our guest was going to carry a black powder gun out in the rain and expect it to go off, if we could even find a gobbler that hadn't floated away. I'd say the odds were about 5000 to 1 that we would do anything but get wet.

Joe was not swayed by our last minute suggestions to wait to see if the rain slacked up. Off we went, Will and I with our lips stuck out and Joe with his black powder shotgun. We waded along until we reached a small clearing that resembled a planted food plot.

Will stopped and yelled in his best thunderstorm voice, "I saw a gobbler strutting here a few days ago. Let's set up and just call for a while."

Joe sat down with his shotgun and faced the opening. The hammers and nipples on the shotgun were covered with plastic wrap. Again, I weighed the odds of Joe getting that sandwich bag off the primers and the gun actually going off. I didn't worry long because deep down any animal would have to be crazy to be out in this storm, much less a wild turkey gobbler.

Will stuck a hen decoy in the clearing and we sat down behind Joe. Will looked at me and shrugged his shoulders and began calling. I joined with the tube call. I'll have to admit it was kind of entertaining to watch the air from the tube call hit the water running off the bill of my cap. It made a nice sort of spray that was fun to watch. Sort of like watching your breath on a cold morning, only wetter. For several minutes we called as loud as possible, but I was sure the rain noise was keeping our calling from traveling very far.

At one point I remember asking Will, "Do you think Joe can hear us?"

Will responded, "I hope so he's only 10 feet away."

Before we could laugh at Will's remark, the black powder gun roared. Will and I must have jumped three feet straight in the air. My first thought was, "My gosh, he's shot himself."

I just knew the sandwich bags he had placed over the percussion primers had caused some type of explosion. By the time we were upright and turning around, I heard Will say, "I don't believe it, it's a gobbler."

Sure enough Joe was calmly walking out to a huge old wet gobbler that was flopping right by the decoy. Surely this must be a dream.

When I reached down to look at the gobbler's spurs, I knew it wasn't a dream. A great gobbler, and what a story for Joe Byers. I was stunned to say the least. Joe's reaction was "good job boys lets take some photos".

Joe did not understand that Will and I had just used every ounce of luck we had saved for the entire season, maybe two seasons. This was a miracle gobbler, the biggest turkey-hunting miracle I had ever seen or even heard about.

Joe went about his business and soon the hunt and photo session was over. As Will folded his decoy, Joe wandered over in the direction the gobbler had appeared from. He motioned us over and said, "Check this out."

There, exactly where the turkey had come from, was a raging creek every bit of 20 feet across and several feet deep. Not only had he come in during a pouring rain, he had flown a creek to do so. My heart dropped as I started figuring how much luck had been severed from my allotment for this to have happened. The way I had it figured I wouldn't hear another turkey for about a year. Joe took a few pictures of the creek and started back toward camp with the huge old wet gobbler on his shoulder. He smiled and asked, "What you boys going to do tomorrow to top this?"

Being a lifelong believer in superstitions, I already knew what sort of day we would have tomorrow, but didn't want to spoil it for Joe. He was well educated, and I'm sure not a believer in the mysterious ways of the turkey gods. I opted for a small smile and prayed that the turkey gods may not have witnessed the miracle. For the next two days Will, Joe and I (the believer) hunted some of the most gorgeous turkey woods on the planet. The wind was calm, the birds were chirping and for ten hours a day we walked and called and called and walked. We didn't set up much because a mosquito hatch had mysteriously taken place that could only be described as a plague. They were relentless. I have never seen them so bad for so long. They would get into any area left exposed.

During all the swatting and swinging trying to keep the bugs off, I let my usually sharp guard down and walked up on a rather large cottonmouth moccasin. I knew then that the turkey gods had indeed seen the miracle gobbler and it was now pay back time.

Needless to say, Joe did not have another hunt and, in my opinion, was lucky to have made it back to his home state of Maryland without an accident.

Whether or not luck plays a role in turkey hunting is not even up for discussion with me. I know it does. I have lucky socks, a lucky hat, and countless rituals that I pay attention to. For example, if someone throws a hat on his or her bed, I'm out of there. I won't go hunting with them, won't stand by them or even talk to them for a while. For me, it goes way beyond the black cat crossing the road. I'm up on most all of the well known and many of the not so well-know superstitions.

Once again Bent Creek Lodge makes a memory. My youngest daughter, Lauran, with her first gobbler. Without question the most excited I've ever been during and after a hunt.

I have had many clear instances where a sign from above paid off either in a positive or negative fashion.

In April of 1995, I was once again on an extended trip in Texas. That particular season on that particular ranch had not been typical Texas hunting. Drought conditions and a constant wind had us hunting hard. The dust factor had my video camera on the brink of failure and lack of sleep had me all but ready to head home.

On the next to last day of the hunt, I was going to film an outdoor writer during an afternoon cutt and run hike. At the last minute, I decided the heck with the camera; I'll just go along and call. Just before I stepped in the truck to head out, I looked down and saw a penny, "heads up" lying on the ground. I picked it up and thought it would take more than a dusty penny to change my luck. The outdoor writer and I headed to a distant windmill and even before we made it to our spot, I heard a gobble. The wind had died down and conditions were getting right in a hurry.

We made it to the windmill and set up under a small, shady live oak tree. One series of calls was answered quickly and, in less than five minutes, a gobbler was in sight. I was already thinking about my video camera that I left in camp. What happened next was a sign as sure as can be. This gobbler eased his way toward a concrete tank that was catching water from the windmill. From the other side, this gobbler jumped or flew up on the top of the narrow rim of the tank and strutted half way around the tank. What unbelievable footage this would have been. The absolute chance of a lifetime to video a gobblers strutting on a 6 inch wide wall for the whole world to see. This gobbler hopped down and proceeded to come within 10 yards of our set up. Both of us were so impressed with his display of vigor and balance that we simply let him walk away. Now you tell me if that heads up penny was a sign.

One of the most unforgettable signs I ever witnessed happened while hunting with my youngest daughter in Alabama. We were hunting on Enon Plantation near Union Springs with Fred Law. Fred is a lifelong turkey hunter and knows exactly how to play the game. It was opening weekend and once again, the weather was trying to dampen an otherwise exciting weekend. Lauran had taken a turkey the previous season and it was one of those five-minute straight-off-the-roost gobblers. She had a memorable hunt, but still hadn't sampled what turkey hunting is all about. On her second venture it was shaping up to be a real learning experience. At dawn, the clouds were thick and gray. The wind howled, so naturally we heard no gobbling at sunrise. So we started the task of walking, calling in the wind lulls and hoping.

The day ended as it started with no encounters at all. The next morning was an exact repeat of the day before. Clouds, occasional rain drops and wind. Once again we were on the move. Lauran and Fred's spirits never wavered. For three hours we moved and called and listened and hoped. At one of our last locations, I was fiddling with my camera while Fred called and glassed from a hilltop. Lauran tapped me on the shoulder and pointed to the west. I turned to see what she had spotted and was amazed to see a dim but definite rainbow peaking through the clouds. Lauran smiled and said maybe the weather would break before we had to head home. At that instant, Fred came running up with a smile from ear to ear.

"I spotted four gobblers across the creek coming into a greenfield," he said. "Let's go."

We jumped in the truck and drove a mile or so to get around the creek. After some crawling and calling, Lauran smacked a nice long beard with my ever-present video camera saving the memory. It was without question one of the most special hunts I have ever witnessed. Did the rainbow mean good luck? You'd have a hard time convincing the three of us that it didn't turn the tables.

Keeping an eye out for four leaf clovers, heads up pennies or rainbows isn't always high on most turkey hunters' priority lists. Truthfully, I don't always wear my lucky hat or my lucky socks. I do watch out for black cats, hats on the bed and such but in the end, I think superstitions just add to the experience. It's one more thing to talk about when you're sharing the outdoors with friends and one of the greatest creatures in the world.

Focus on the Hunt

Of all the fond memories I have of spring turkey hunting, by far the most cherished seem to involve filming. I have been blessed to be able to share hundreds of hunts and encounters with strangers through the magic of videotape. It has been more fun and more rewarding than I ever imagined. It has been the continuous driving force that has prompted me to carry 60 pounds of gear each step I make during hunting season.

I have no regrets and can honestly say that if not for a video camera and what I've been able to record over the years, it's pretty certain that no one in the hunting world would know my name. As much as I have enjoyed that extra 60 pounds over the past 15 years, not all of the memories were funny at the time. When you're recording hunts for a living, the stress level can go up a notch. The early years were especially stressful. When you're learning the equipment as well as about how to get it into hunting situations without breaking it, drowning it, dropping it or losing it, well, like I said, it can be stressful.

Over the years the cameras have become lighter, more portable and easier to use. The early cameras were none of the above. Heavy, loud, and complicated may be the best words to describe the first camera I used professionally. Add to this the fact that Primos Game Calls was a fledgling company and this camera was a huge investment, which made the stress level extremely high. This stress level peaked one day when I managed to totally loose this huge, heavy, loud and very expensive camera in the middle of the woods.

I was with my friend, Ross McGhee, who helped Will and me while we were making the first "Truth" video. Ross had some prime land near Natchez, Mississippi, and was always willing to help put us on a gobbling turkey. This hunt involved an outdoor writer who was making one of his first trips down south. Ross had roosted a gobbler in the evening and offered to guide the writer while I recorded the hunt. The plan worked to perfection until the gun went off.

The shot was a bit low and the gobbler rolled, ran, stumbled, flew and flopped out of view. At this point, we're all off and running after the gobbler that was hit hard whether he knew it or not. The chase was one I'll never forget. It turned into a two-hour ordeal and covered about a quarter of a mile. The terrain included hills and hollows, briars and bushes, creek bottoms and bluffs. The gobbler finally was spotted peaking from a small ditch and was dispatched once and for all. The celebration was huge. What a find after covering so much ground.

It was story material for the writer and quite a good hunt on tape, at least up until the shot was fired. I was anxious to look at the footage and started back to the scene of the crime.

You would have to know the area we were in to appreciate the next few hours. The huge, heavy, loud, expensive camera that was covered totally in Mossy Oak was nowhere to be found. We backtracked, re-tracked and new tracked and still no camera. We were having trouble finding the exact spot where we had set up and, for the first 30 minutes, it was kind of funny. Two hours later it wasn't funny at all.

We walked and walked and still could not find the camera. Finally Ross located the exact spot and still no camera. I was convinced someone had heard the commotion, came onto the spot and made off with the camera.

I sat down and began to conjure up a tale that I could relay back to Will Primos. Just as my story was coming together Ross without saying a word began laughing and pointing. I stood up and walked to the spot where he was pointing and there on its side lay the heavy, loud and complicated camera. It had apparently fallen over when I jumped up and had landed in a small depression. That along with the Mossy Oak camo job had it hidden in plain sight.

I was never so glad to strap the 60-pound camera on my shoulder. I never even told Will Primos about the almost lost camera. I guess he'll know now.

Today there are countless video cameras in the woods each spring. Now more than ever, people are carrying camcorders into the field and making their own movies. There is no better way to share the memory than to simply pop the tape in your TV. Over the years I have done many seminars on how to video your hunt, so I know first hand how many people are truly interested in doing it.

There are a few tips that can make your outdoor movies better and may even encourage you to take your amateur filming to the next level.

The first thing you'll need to do is make a commitment. I have learned and proven time and again that you can't concentrate on shooting with two things at one time. If you truly want to video tape a hunt, you must dedicate yourself to that goal. You'll need to become a cameraman. This doesn't mean that you'll have to give up your hunting. Try the buddy system, film one trip and then hunt the next. You'll soon learn that getting a hunt on tape is as much fun and just as exciting as pulling the trigger. I can assure you that it is much harder to capture the hunt on tape than to just shoot a gobbler. The challenge is great and so are the rewards.

There are some other things to consider when you decide to start videotaping your hunts. Don't get burned out too soon. If the camera becomes a ball and chain and you're not having fun, leave it at home. Remember that every day in the woods is a blessing and you should enjoy it to the fullest.

When you make the decision to carry the camera and you want to get serious about your results, then there are some things that can aid greatly in the amount of footage you get and the quality. Gaining access to good places is a key to getting good footage. I have the pleasure of working every day with some of the best hunters in the nation. From Toxey Haas to each member of the TV crew, who we call the camo cameras, these people will tell you it's all about geography. Get the word out in your area that you're filming and you might be surprised with the invitations you receive. Places that were off limits before can become accessible.

Don't be afraid to talk to landowners to gain access. All landowners like to know they are good stewards of the land. If you get on a piece of land and get some footage, show it to the landowner. You may develop a relationship that will last for years. Offer to take them or their friends or family on a hunt.

Check out "NO HUNTING" areas such as wildlife refuges and state parks. Many of these areas will let you hunt with a camera, but be sure and ask permission beforehand. These no hunting areas can be a gold mine for footage. You can't hunt with a gun, but you can call and have a chance at some rare footage that can be hard to get in areas where turkeys are hunted regularly.

If you don't already have a video camera, then picking the right one depends on what you're going to do with it. If your goal is to just film occasionally and use it for all the normal family things, then any camera will do. If you think you might one day want to produce a video or have commercial aspirations, then some thought needs to go into this decision. Today video cameras are so good that almost any consumer grade camera will shoot footage of a quality high enough to produce a video. Digital cameras produce footage of an especially high quality and are available in many price ranges.

We have signs in all of our edit rooms at Mossy Oak that read, "If your video doesn't sound good, it doesn't look good."

If you want your video to really take on a professional look, purchase a good remote microphone. Make sure your camera has a remote microphone jack. Find a microphone that is omni-directional and has at least a ten-foot cord. This will enable you to pick up all the natural sound and loose the mechanical noise that is common with cameras and their built-in microphones.

Next, buy a tripod. Get one that has a fluid or imitation fluid head for smooth pans and moves. Look for one that does not have braces between the legs. You'll need to pull the tripod in close when sitting down and braces will hamper you in doing this. Once you've got your equipment list complete, here are some tips that will get you up to speed and have your footage looking professional in a hurry.

Practice before the season on small game. Spend time outdoors trying to film birds, squirrels, cats and dogs. This will get you familiar with your camera and some of the moves you'll need to make in the field.

Always run your camera in the manual focus mode. This will keep the camera from focusing on twigs or bushes that may be in between you and the subject you are trying to film.

Try to keep from zooming in and out too much. This type of footage will make the viewer seasick. Center the subject and keep it framed. Think of your viewfinder as a small TV and frame your shot as though you are watching TV at home. Once you get comfortable with the camera, then here are some other pointers that will make the actual hunt footage better.

First, always shoot more footage than you think you'll need. Shoot everything from hunters getting ready to hunters setting up to walking in the woods. Pay attention to the scenery and look for shots that will help show the viewers where you were. Tell a story. You can worry about what shots to keep and which to lose later. Try to get the hunter's reactions before, during and after the hunt. Have him talk to you about where he was, what he was doing and why. All of this will help add to the final product.

Finally, if you get a complete hunt on tape, make sure the impact and the recovery are shown in a tasteful manner. Take a few minutes and think about how to show this part of the hunt. Make sure to show proper respect to the animal, as his contribution to the hunt was far greater than yours.

In the end, what you have done is captured a memory that will last for a lifetime. If the excitement level for you was high and the reward of capturing the hunt and the emotions were more than you expected, then you're lucky. You may have found a way to share you're love of the outdoors and the wild turkey with thousands of people who would never get a look into your world.

Bent Creek Lodge in Alabama was the site for my first successful outdoor writers' hunt as Mossy Oak's PR guy. It's still my favorite place in the world to hunt and hang out.

God Bless the Neophytes

Lord knows the mistakes I made early on while hunting turkeys could be a book in itself. Like any other turkey hunter I still make mistakes, but today I know how to keep them to myself, or at least conceal them better.

In any sport, the beginning years are a combination of nerves, mistakes, blunders and "what ifs," but in turkey hunting, the mistakes seem to stick in your memory for a much longer period of time. I don't know if this is because the emotion level is so high or just your mind works in high gear when things go south on a turkey hunt.

Whatever the reason, blunders made during a turkey hunt are often burned into the memory of the hunter. They are certainly burned into the memory of anyone who may have witnessed the incident. It never fails that when you seem to make that once in a lifetime error in judgment, someone is always there to witness it. It then becomes story fodder for years to come. Some of the best stories about beginners come from seasoned veterans who take much pride in embarrassing a new hunter. Once this loud-mouthed know-it-all gets some information he feels might be funny, he'll take any and all opportunities to tell the story to anyone who might listen.

I have always been hesitant to haul off and embarrass anyone. Sure, I tell more than my share of amusing tales about rookie hunters, but I will always wait until the person in question is not in attendance. Most times I will leave his name out to keep the rookie from getting discouraged and moving on to another sport. In some rare cases, the story of stories will come first hand, from the person who actually committed the act. When you witness one of these first hand accounts; it's a rare and wonderful treat. You should hang on every word and relish the moment. If at all possible, wait until the conclusion of the tale to laugh.

Make this person feel good about sharing their experience and be supportive. Tell them something similar has happened to you or some other hunter. Pay close attention so you can use the story later. You can add and exaggerate, stretch and make up things making the tale truly world class. As long as the tales are all in good fun, then hey let the games begin.

One of my favorite stories about a neophyte took place in Alabama in 1988. I was going to take these two fellows to Bent Creek Lodge near Jachin, Alabama. I have had so many great hunts and good fun at Bent Creek that I could talk about them for hours. I'll make it short by just stating that they have some of the best turkey hunting in the South and, without question, some of the finest guides in the nation. These guides are successful year after year while hunting the same sections of land day after day. Anyone can call up an unpressured two-year-old, but hunting the same turkeys for days on end and killing some takes a truly talented and patient individual.

Back to the Neophytes. I met these two guys who were seasoned deer hunters but had never turkey hunted. They were in the right place to gain vast amounts of knowledge from the Bent Creek guides. For one entire evening the guides schooled these old boys on how to sit down and keep your gun steady and still. The art of calling and crawling and when to do both. How to sneak up on a field without getting busted. School was in and it was awesome. I don't think either of these two fellows slept a wink that night. They were truly excited and ready to experience their first spring hunt.

The next morning I went with Bent Creek guide Bob Walker. Bob would guide one of the hunters while I videotaped the hunt. Nothing like a neophyte to make a movie more exciting. The drive to our listening spot was about 25 minutes and not once did the new hunter shut up. He had a dozen things to go over with Bob and me about what would take place.

He was making sure he knew the plan and what he should do in any situation. Once we arrived at our listening post, Bob and I were standing about 30 yards apart straining our ears for a gobble. The new hunter was all smiles and busting at the seams to get this thing underway. After several minutes of listening with not a peep from the wood line, Bob let out one of his totally realistic owl hoots. When the neophyte heard this owl sound he ran over to Bob and grabbed his shirtsleeve and in a panicked voice said, "Hey, I thought we were going to hunt turkeys." I had to walk off to keep from laughing. Bob, being his normal cool self, explained the owl hooting, response theory, and the hunt continued.

I love taking hunters who are experienced in other aspects of the hunting world but are still neophytes when it comes to turkeys. So many times you try and relay information about what to do or what to expect only to be cut off in mid sentence with a "Hey, this ain't my first rodeo" sort of response.

When this happens two or three times in the early stages of the hunt, then the pressure's off as far as guiding this person. All you have to do is call and sit back. Not a bad gig. Such was the case with a fellow I took one spring near my home. This guy was a big deal in the sporting goods industry and an extremely nice guy. He was also an experienced hunter, except with turkeys. I began to explain the plan for the afternoon and got that "This ain't my first rodeo" comment. From that point on, I just kind of shut up.

I went to an area where this old gobbler had been hanging out. I knew the gobbler probably had twenty or more hens with him and would never come to calling, so we set up on this old boy's favorite clover field. One soft yelp on a slate provoked a gobble from just inside the woods and instantly my hunter raised his gun to his shoulder. I knew that by the time something happened, if anything, this fellow's arms would be jelly if he tried to hold that gun up the entire time.

Hey, this wasn't his first rodeo, so I just sat there. Sure enough, this old gobbler came into the field about 200 yards away. He was alone and looked like he wanted to play the game. I was shocked but gathered myself enough to cast another yelp. Immediately the gobbler went into strut and spun around and gobbled back. It was then I got a look at his beard. It was at least 12 inches long with a very non-typical curl in the middle. I thought about taking the gun from the hunter, but he still had it up to his shoulder. Even now this fellow was starting to wiggle a bit from the weight of the gun. His breathing was heavy and the sweat was starting to run down his neck. For the next 10 minutes this old gobbler strutted and spun and pecked and gobbled but moved only about 50 yards. By now the hunter was soaking wet and the gun was spinning around more than the strutting gobbler. Finally the gobbler committed. He began his walk in our direction and did not stop until he was a mere 25 yards from the hunter. I whispered for him to shoot. Nothing. I whispered again "shoot him". Nothing. Finally my whispering turned to desperation volume and the gobbler caught on. He did the "leaving call" and trotted away. I looked at the hunter in time to see him let go of the gun and fall back on the ground. His glasses were fogged with perspiration so badly that condensation had completely covered both lenses. He could not see anything. Even the thought of that once in a lifetime chance at a once in a lifetime gobbler could not keep me from laughing at the sight of this guy arms cramped and glasses covered in sweat laying on the ground. If only he hadn't told me twice "This ain't my first rodeo," I could have saved him from such an ordeal.

My all time favorite neophyte tale took place in the mid 80s and happened with a bonified seasoned veteran hunter in the group. This big time hunter was guiding a neophyte on what I believe was his second or third turkey hunt.

The experienced hunter had taken this guy under his wing and was introducing him to the ways of wary gobblers. The hunt in question started off innocently enough. No gobbling at daybreak followed by walking and calling. They were on some new property, so the experienced hunter wanted to cover every inch and leave no stone unturned. About 9 a.m. the seasoned hunter pulled out his paddleboat box call signed by the maker and ran off a series of loud sharp yelps. From as far away as you could hear, a gobble echoed back from the east. Finally a gobbler that might play the game.

After a few more calls and several hundred yards, the hunters set up and began stage two of the hunt. At first the gobbler answered any call the experienced hunter made. Soon the gobbler would only answer to loud cutts and yelps on the paddleboat call signed by the maker. The seasoned hunter decided they needed to move close, which they did.

Stage three was now underway. Again the gobbler started responding to any call. Thirty minutes later he would only answer to loud cutts. After some head scratching and deep thought, the hunters decided to move one more time and call from another direction.

Stage four was now underway. By the fourth set up it was nearly 11 o'clock and the gobbler was still fired up. Again the same results. The seasoned hunter was pulling tricks from his bag that must have amazed the neophyte. He climbed a tree and determined there was a field ahead and the gobbler must be strutting with hens. The seasoned hunter decided a sneak was the only option left. The gobbler had not moved much if at all, so they would have to go to him.

Stage five was now unfolding. After 45 minutes and almost 150 yards, the hunters, from their bellies, could see a clearing ahead. The seasoned hunter gave directions on what would take place now. He picked his assault path and told the neophyte to crawl low in front and he would stay right behind him. With a final landmark picked for the rise and shoot, the two crawled forward.

Once the landmark was reached, the seasoned hunter told the neophyte, "Get your gun ready and raise up slowly. Find the gobbler and shoot before he sees you."

With the stealth of a Marine Corps sniper, the neophyte slowly raised up shouldering his gun the entire way. The seasoned hunter waited with gleaming anticipation but no shot. He turned to see the neophyte starring into the clearing and asked, "Do you see him?"

"Nope," replied the neophyte.

"What can you see?" was the next whisper.

The next words from the neophyte will live with this veteran hunter for life.

"I see a woman hanging her drawers on a clothes line."

The experienced hunter raised up to see a small country house, complete with clothes line, water well, tin roof, and a big old tame gobbler sitting on the chicken coop, still strutting.

I'd be willing to bet that this isn't the only case in history of someone sneaking up on a yard gobbler. Back in those days, many country homes had a big tom strutting around the barnyard. I myself came close to falling for this apparition one spring morning. Luckily I figured out what was going on just in the knick of time. Besides I was hunting alone and would never have told anyone that I whacked a very ugly 33-pound gobbler with a head the size of mine.

Hunting on public land with other turkey hunters will make you a better hunter. It will also make you appreciate the wariness of pressured gobblers.

Pressured Birds On Public Land

There I was, standing by my two-ton milk truck in the middle of nowhere.

I had just put on my camo coveralls and was reaching for my twelve gauge when the car skidded to a stop next to me.

"Got any fresh buttermilk," the lady asked. "No Ma'am, all out today," I replied.

You would think the sight of an extra large milkman in camo holding a shotgun would seem a bit odd to most folks, but apparently this lady had seen my red and brown milk truck in rural Adams County before. The fact that I was parked on the Sandy Creek Wildlife Management Area in southwest Mississippi during turkey season was not all that strange. Back in the early 70s, I was delivering milk and I strategically planned my route to end up near the Sandy Creek WMA at least twice a week.

After the lady with a craving for buttermilk left, I slipped on my boots and headed down Pretty Creek Road. It was 3 p.m. and no other hunters were ever in the WMA that time of the day. I stopped and stroked my box call every few hundred yards and on the third or fourth sequence, a gobbler answered. He sounded no more than 200 yards to the west. I made my way into the hardwood bottom and set up next to a tall beech tree. Before I could get set up and ready the gobbler hammered away twice. He was on his way.

I decided to call once more before raising the gun. I scratched out my best imitation of a hen yelp, and again, the gobbler answered. The booming echo of the gobble was still bouncing in the hardwoods when I saw the gobbler at approximately 40 yards. He was not strutting but trotting in my direction. At 25 yards, I took the shot and the gobbler folded.

I remember thinking two things as I walked back to my milk truck that afternoon. One, I may never have an easier hunt than the one I just enjoyed. Two, I need to load up some extra buttermilk for tomorrow.

Turkey hunts like the one I enjoyed that day are rare. On

public hunting ground, they can be extremely rare. Fifteen to twenty years ago, hunting pressure was light during the spring season. Turkeys were not as plentiful back then, so an easy hunt was still something to relish. Today, the hunter that cruises public grounds during spring gobbler season must have a big bag of tricks and be willing to put in the extra effort needed to bag high-pressure birds.

One of my old hunting buddies had a name for gobblers on public lands; he called them politicians. He said they would promise you a lot and give you very little. He learned that during late February and early March, gobblers on the public land he hunted would gobble like mad. By the time the season opened, a combination of hunters owling and calling from the main roads trying to locate would shut the gobblers down for the most part. This early gobbling would let you know the birds were there, but once hunting season started you could not find one, kind of like looking for your congressman after the election.

Bob Dixon, Vice President of New Business Development at Mossy Oak Camouflage, grew up hunting gobblers on public lands around Birmingham, Alabama. Bob has many competitive turkey calling and owling titles to his credit, and admits hunting on public land made him a much better turkey hunter. Bob hunted what he called MMA gobblers, (Major Metropolitan Area).

According to Bob, "The areas around Birmingham held good numbers of wild turkeys. There was U.S. Steel property, Kimberly Clark Paper Company land and several Alabama State Management areas to hunt. Back in the late 70s, there were fewer turkey hunters, but in the Birmingham area, there were enough die hard hunters to make public grounds a challenge".

Bob learned the hard way that pressured gobblers require some special tactics.

He explains, "Turkey woods close to home are a blessing and a curse. The fact that you can go out and hunt an hour or so before work makes your season better with more chances to bag a gobbler. It also offers that same plus to other hunters in the area. If you have turkey woods close to a populated area, you better be ready to share those spots with other hunters."

Bob learned that many hunters on public ground would listen from the main roads and go to the gobblers from the same directions.

He also was guilty of this on many occasions until he figured out that going to the gobblers from another direction was his best move.

He continues, "After a few years of watching and listening to gobblers and hunters in some of the high pressured spots, I learned that coming in to the gobbler from behind was a good move. Hunters would almost always owl and locate from the main roads and then walk straight in set up to call. I would set up in hopes of the gobblers moving away from the roads and the constant calling of other hunters. This was probably the best tactic I found that worked on gobblers that were called to and hunted virtually every day of the season."

Leaving the main roads and taking the time to maneuver in behind the gobblers takes some extra effort, but extra effort is what hunting public land gobblers is all about. Bob's circling tactic was one of his best tricks for heavy hunted grounds, but it wasn't his only trick. Bob confesses that no matter where you set up on some gobblers, they are just too spooky in the morning to be huntable. After many mornings of hearing all the traffic, yelping, cackling, owling and being spooked out of the trees, turkeys will often just sit in the trees longer, remain silent and wait for the woods to quiet down before going about their routine.

According to Bob, "The best tactic to use when pressure really gets heavy is to hunt in the afternoon, if it is legal in your state. This technique is different, but the results can be rewarding."

Bob has told me for years that if he had to choose one part of the day and could only hunt that half, he would take noon until dark without question. He has always been an all-day hunter and realized that hunting in the afternoon was a needed part of hunting on public land. He said, "Looking back, I can say without a doubt, that the majority of the gobblers I took on public land were later in the day, say 10 a.m. to 2 p.m. I know this was because hunting pressure was low during those hours."

Today, Bob hunts mainly on private land. He has taken all four species of turkeys found in the U.S., and told me his early years hunting on public ground made him a much better turkey hunter.

He says, "if you can consistently take gobblers on public ground, you will have learned the hard way. Hunts on less pressured gobblers will be much easier once you have had to match wits not only with a smart old gobbler, but a few dozen hunters at the same time".

Down in Dixie is not the only place you will find public ground with a hunter or two on every ridge during the spring. Paul Newsom of Oklahoma City, Oklahoma, has been hunting public gobblers for many years and has shared his hunting ground with many other hunters.

Paul is best known to the public as a spokesman for the National Rifle Association. He is the host of the highly successful NRA American Hunters Tour as well as one of the featured speakers for those events. He has been featured in many NRA television commercials and has produced several videos on hunting. He has hunted virtually all species of game animals in the U.S., but his first love and passion is wild turkeys.

Paul had the luxury in his home state of hunting three species of wild turkeys: the Eastern, Rio Grande and Merriam. He has taken what he calls the Oklahoma Slam more than once, and let me know quickly that any species of wild turkey can be tough when the pressure gets hot and heavy.

He explains, "I learned early on that the easiest places to get to were always the hardest hunted. I have always been aggressive when it came to collecting the MRI (most recent information) on certain areas. Often times, just a conversation with a game warden or local resident will guide you into areas less visited by hunters. Don't be shy when it comes to asking questions. I always look for an opening to start a conversation with someone who might know where turkeys are located. It may be in a store, cafe or gas station. Most of the public lands in Oklahoma are large tracks that can cover more than one county. Most people will volunteer information on where they see turkeys, especially if they are not a turkey hunter. This can help you start your hunting or scouting in a good area."

Paul's tactics for public gobblers were very similar to Bob's when it came to putting the odds in your favor. He too prefers hunting mid-day and afternoons. He also likes weekdays as opposed to weekends.

"If you can afford to hunt all day during the week, public lands can be just as productive as any private ground. Most people cannot adjust their work schedule to do this. I have been lucky enough to find many weekdays to hunt and have found little competition during the week. The only exception to this is often the first week of the season when some hunters will take vacation time to spend all week in the field."

Paul believes another tactic that works well on public ground is creative locating. Paying attention to what other hunters are doing to locate gobblers will tell you what not to do.

He explains, "I have found that most hunters will owl, crow or use loud yelps and cackles to try and get a response from a gobbler.

One of my favorite calls to use when locating in the morning while gobblers are on the roost is a coyote howler. This call seems to work very well while the gobblers are still in the trees. They may not respond to it as well once they have flown down, but early in the morning it works great."

One of Paul's best tips is on patience. He believes pressured gobblers come in silent most of the time. According to Paul, "not only do many gobblers on heavy hunting ground come in silent, they take much longer to come to your calling. They may have been called too many other times by hunters and have learned to approach cautiously. Once I get a gobbler to respond and I set up, I make sure I am very comfortable because I may give this set up an hour or more before moving. I use soft yelps and feeding calls and call very little if I feel the gobbler is in fairly close. Listen for drumming while you are set up. That may be all you hear before a gobbler shows up."

Another tactic Paul has used successfully on public ground, especially late in the season, is gobbling. He stresses this tactic should not be used under any circumstances if you feel there are other hunters in the area, and only if you are set up properly. He feels a gobble in the right situation can bring in many old gobblers.

He explains, "first you must remember that this call should only be a last resort. You must be set up with your back against a tree larger than your outline. If you try this with a commercial call that requires lots of movement, be careful. I gobble with my natural voice and make an extra effort not to move when I gobble."

Paul feels this call can work in certain situations much like antler rattling works on whitetails. Whether it's territorial or social, Paul has had this tactic pay off more than once while hunting pressured gobblers.

On one such occasion, Paul was hunting the Quachita National Forest in Southeast Oklahoma. He recalls, "It was late in the season and I had worked a gobbler for two hours in the morning but never got him in close enough for a clean shot. I was on my way back to camp and decided to stop and rest a while. I set up near a clearing on top of a mountain. The clearing was once a helipad used by the Forest Service Fire Fighters. I decided to take a break for a while and have a snack.

"I set up facing down the mountain and went ahead and cast a few yelps before pulling out my candy bar. On the first series of calls I had no response. I waited about fifteen minutes and called again. This time I heard a gobble down the mountain, a little to my right. I was quiet for a while and I never heard the gobbler again. About 20 minutes passed and I saw the gobbler moving from my right to left, still about 300 yards down the mountain. I called once more with no response. I knew I did not have time to get in front of the gobbler because of the open terrain in which he was traveling.' "Since I had not seen another hunter in three full days of hunting the Quachita National Forest, I decided to gobble once just to see if I could get a response. I did my best impression of a full roll gobble and the gobbler responded with a double gobble. I waited for a few minutes and the gobbler gobbled on his own somewhat closer. I decided to remain silent. A few minutes passed before I saw the white crown of the gobbler at 35 yards making his way up the mountain. I was able to move my gun in position and took the gobbler at 25 yards. The 22-pound gobbler sported a 10-inch beard and curved one-inch spurs. Like it or not, the gobble brought that tom in when nothing else would work."

Just being creative can help when chasing gobblers on public land. The fellow that taught me how to turkey hunt had a saying for every situation. His favorite about turkey hunting was, "Son, there are absolutely no absolutes when hunting turkeys." Keep that in mind when you're hunting turkeys on public ground. Be safe and be creative.

Cuttin' and Runnin'

The sounds of the loud yelp were still echoing in the woods when the caller leaned down to tie his bootlace. It was almost 11 a.m. and the pause seemed like stop number 100 on an endless walk through the countryside. To that point, I had only watched and listened as the well-known turkey caller guided the outdoor writer through the morning. While the guide was still lacing his boot, I pulled out my tube call.

I did a short but very loud cutt and from the timber a faint but distinct gobbler returned the salute. Our trio hotfooted it a couple hundred yards in the direction of the gobbler and set up. Our caller-slash-guide went to work with some sweet sounds that were more than enough to trick any old gobbler. Moments later, the red, white and blue head appeared and was soon greeted by a single shotgun blast.

This scenario has taken place with me countless times over the years. The strange looks you get from other hunters when you blast a loud locator call will turn to smiles if a gobbler answers in the distance. I learned how to hunt gobblers the old fashion way. You called very little and sat still a lot. I still use this tactic today, but do a lot more moving and calling depending on the situation.

Knowing what call to make and when to move on a gobbler is probably the toughest thing for beginning turkey hunters to figure out. No turkey hunter, no matter how famous, well known or experienced, makes this decision correctly every time.

Experience and confidence will help you decide when to move on a gobbler. There are a few situations that dictate moving fairly fast. For instance, you are set up on a gobbler that is gobbling in the tree. You hear hens yelping and flying down near by.

The turkey continues to gobble after he has flown down, but is moving away. It doesn't take a rocket scientist to realize the gobbler has hens and is paying no attention to your calling. Remember, the best caller in the world is just another hen in the woods. If you can keep the tom gobbling with a loud yelp or cackle, then try and

Once, I left home at 3:30 a.m. without my tube call. I drove back 53 miles to get it. I don't leave home without it.

get in front of the flock.

You also might consider moving to another area and coming back to your original spot later in the morning.

Another situation that might require moving is in the case of a gobbler that keeps gobbling in the same place. If a tom is gobbling to your calling but not coming in, a number of things could be holding or hanging him up. It may be a barrier like a creek or fence. If you are familiar with the area and realize he is hung up due to an obstacle, shut up calling.

If the gobbler has hens with him, you will often have more luck later in the day. Hens may leave the gobbler to start nesting, and a lonesome gobbler is much easier to call into gun range.

Moving or hunting more aggressively for gobblers requires some special tactics. Camouflage is very important in any turkey-hunting situation, but when moving and setting up in a hurry, you need to have total confidence in your camo. The mix and match system from Mossy Oak works great under these conditions. It will not only blend into your surroundings, but will also break your outline.

Try to set up in the shade if possible, and make sure all shinny objects, including your gun, are covered.

When moving and calling or "cuttin' and runnin'," again there is no absolute best way to do it. There are generally two schools of thought on how to locate gobblers after fly down. The first is to stop in your desired spot and use a locator call such as an owl or crow.

If this does not provoke a gobble, then changing to a soft yelp is usually the next tactic. If this does not work, then its time to give him your best and loudest call to make him gobble.

This type of moving and calling is a great way to cover ground and locate gobblers. The second method is one that I use most of the time, but again, it depends on the general area, how hard it has been hunted and for how long. This method is to basically pick a spot, stop and issue your best, sharpest, loudest call up front. I like to use a tube call and make four or five sharp cutting type notes. This sound carries well and seems to provoke more gobbles than any other method I use. I have had most of my luck dragging a gobble out of a reluctant tom with a tube call. This call makes a loud, sharp note that seems to get a response when nothing else works.

My good friend and life-long turkey hunter Jim Casada uses a wing bone for his locator. How he generates enough volume from a wing bone to carry long distance is a mystery, but I have seen it work first-hand on many occasions. I have a theory on locating gobblers, which is just that, a theory. I believe most gobblers spend most of their time during the spring with hens. The gobblers spend most of their days listening to soft yelps and clucks and feeding sounds. I believe that a loud sharp cut or yelp will come closer to getting a response than just another soft yelp, crow or owl call in the distance. It probably depends on the gobbler, but I feel that even if it is just one shock gobble, I can get more responses by starting out with a loud sharp turkey call.

My favorite call to use when locating or cuttin' and runnin' is a tube call. I first saw this call hanging around the neck of Will Primos. I thought it odd looking and even more odd sounding, but the results were anything but odd. Will would use the call to make loud cuts and yelps and turkeys seemed to respond well to the high-pitched sound.

I soon realized that using a tube or what some refer to as a "snuff can" call is difficult. I set out to master the call and the early sounds I made were awful. Something between a honking goose and a bleating jackass would be a good comparison.

I continued to practice with the Primos tube call and became efficient. To this day, I can generate more volume with this call than any other device. I can honestly say that this one call has affected my turkey hunting more than anything else I've ever run across. I'm not sure if it's the sharp pitch or the shear volume that makes this call such a good locator, but the results over the years have been amazing. I can't tell you how many times I've been hunting with someone and made a turkey gobble after they have gone through an entire routine on whatever calls they use to locate. My faith in the tube call to make a turkey gobble has made me hunt harder and longer during the day and has resulted in countless encounters with mid-day gobblers.

As much as I prefer the tube call, believe me it's not the perfect locator for everyone. It's hard to master and most folks can't generate the volume I'm able to. I think my oversized head acts as a sound chamber or something, but for whatever reason, for me, it's deadly.

All successful turkey hunters have a favorite locator call that they have learned will provoke a gobble. Slates, box calls or mouth calls will work. It's all about having confidence and generating volume. This volume is where the term calling too much and too loud probably came from. I've heard it for two decades. Even though I only use the tube call for long distance locating, not calling in a gobbler, people still love to shake their heads and tell me I'm scaring the turkeys to death. Whatever type of loud, long-distance locator you choose, often times you'll get one shock gobble response and that's it. If that's the case, at least you know there's a gobbler nearby and you can move in that direction, set up and then start your normal calling routine.

This happens a lot and there are a couple of ways to address this problem. One is to try to make the gobbler sound off another time or two. If he gets fired up enough to respond several times, he may work on in, especially if it's later in the day.

Another way to approach this problem is to simply set up after hearing one gobble, call periodically and wait. If the gobbler you located does not respond, there is always the chance another gobbler is in the area and close enough to hear your calling. There is nothing sneakier than a silent gobbler.

When you set up to call, whether you have made a turkey gobble or not, assume that your calls are being heard and sooner or later a gobbler will come in. Don't move much and keep a sharp eye for any movement. It's also wise to assume another hunter may sneak into your set up. If this happens, don't shout or wave. Speak to the hunter in a normal voice, "Hey, I'm over here."

Another safety point should be mentioned here. Never walk and call at the same time. When covering ground to move or try and locate a gobbler, stop and set up before calling. You might want to wear a small piece of hunter orange while moving around in the turkey woods.

This spring, if you are set up calling and think you should move on a gobbler or just change areas, do it. Be careful while moving in the turkey woods, but cover some ground and be aggressive.

Lack of Sleep Can Make You Crazy

Only a true veteran turkey hunter can understand what sleep deprivation can actually do to the human body, mind and spirit. Of all the humorous, embarrassing and unbelievable moments that go along with the all-out battle of spring, nothing rates higher on the laughter scale than mind numb, camo clad adults walking around like zombies. I am truly surprised that this country has not had a legitimate disaster because of this problem. I do suspect that if you investigated every train wreck, plane crash, fender bender, house fire and black out in the country you could find in at least some cases where a worn-out turkey hunter was asleep at the wheel, so to speak.

My own personal experiences with this zombie like behavior are numerous. In one week during the 1987 season, I almost lost my wife twice and burned down a house. I can only imagine on a national scale the close calls that have gone without public knowledge.

In the spring of 1987, I was doing battle with some of the worst turkeys in Mississippi. To make matters even more stressful, I was carrying 72 pounds of camera gear and following Will Primos who, at the time, weighed about 160 pounds and was in great shape.

It was a program that Jenny Craig would have been proud of.

This particular season took 35 pounds off my frame and probably a couple of years off my life. The schedule was relentless. I was operating on three to four hours sleep a night. I would hunt all day and entertain outdoor writers and customers half the night. Toward the end of the season, it all started to catch up with me.

On one particular Thursday afternoon, Will and I had chased an evil, long legged, loud mouthed, running gobbler across half of Copiah County for most of the morning.

Our plan was to clean up the camp, eat and head home for a much needed rest day. Will was inside the camp cleaning up and I was on the front porch preparing a turkey breast for grilling. I built a fire in the grill and sat down in the porch swing to let the flames die down. Will had managed to make it as far as his bed and was asleep in seconds. I too got comfortable in the swing and dozed off. Sometime between REM sleep and all-out snoring, I dreamed there was a fire in the house. I jumped from the swing, turned to the house and was relieved to see Will sleeping like a baby through the window.

Just about that time, I smelled smoke. I turned to my charcoal grill and saw flames shooting 30 feet into the air. My grill had started a small grass fire that made its way to a large pile of pine kindling that was next to an even larger stack of firewood. The firewood was blazing and flames were heading up a telephone pole and over to a pecan tree.

I screamed for Will to bring water as I ran off the porch. I used my camo shirt to beat the flames, which only grew bigger. I turned to see Will headed in my direction with one small glass of water in his hand. When he saw the size of the fire, he looked at the glass and ran back into the house. I figured he was going after a pitcher this time.

Will managed to find a garden hose and together we extinguished the blaze. It was a bit of a close call and really spoiled what could have been a good nap.

That night I arrived home and was really looking forward to sleeping in and spending time with my wife and daughters. What I found at home was a house full of my wife's family and an uncle that was ready to go turkey hunting the next morning. Worse than that, he wanted to stay up and talk about turkey hunting.

My wife reminded me that if I could hunt all season and entertain guests with Will Primos, then I could surely entertain one more guest with a hunt. I did my best to stay up and talk turkey with uncle Louie and only fell asleep once in front of the guest. I was awakened by a stiff elbow to the ribs from my wife who never stopped smiling during this altercation.

The next morning, we were up at 4:30 a.m. and off to the woods. I was glad the woods were silent at daybreak. I owled and crowed, yelped and cutt with no response. I planned on my next stop to be the waffle house. As luck would have it, a turkey gobbled on his own when we were a few hundred yards from the truck. I yelped and once again the hunt was on.

Three-and-a-half hours, three set ups and about a mile later, the gobbler stuck his head over a bush at 20 yards and uncle Louie spooked him by saying, "There he is!" in a voice they probably heard at the Waffle House, which was now serving lunch.

That afternoon we spent walking and calling with no luck. By fly up time, I was exhausted. I got uncle Louie back to my house and collapsed on the couch. Just as I was about to doze off, I got another elbow to the ribs from my wife who was trying to hand me my backyard cooking utensils.

"Fire up the grill and wake up!"

I dragged myself outside and managed to cook 12 chicken quarters for the big family meal. Once the table was set, we all sat down for the meal and Pam told me to bless the table. Before I could bow my head good, Uncle Louie had to give the entire family a play-by-play of the day's hunt. Some where in the middle of the tale, I lost it. My head was already bowed, the chair was comfortable and you guessed it, I went out like a light.

My oldest daughter Amy said that when my wife told me once again to ask the blessing I let out a small nasal sound that could have been confused with a snore. The crowd went silent and I can only guess the expression on my wife's face. The next elbow in the ribs was a mighty blow. It was followed by several days of the silent treatment, and finally a few weeks of constant reminders of how much I had embarrassed the whole family. Needless to say, there were no naps at my house the rest of turkey season.

Even after the "silent prayer," as it came to be known, the relentless schedule of filming turkeys continued. The last week of the season Will Primos and I had two guests in camp. Gobbling turkeys were getting scarce and once again we were covering ground. You have to understand that by this point in the season, I was all but brain dead. I was going through the motions but running out of gas quickly. The last night in camp, we cooked and talked and looked at videotape until late into the night. Once our guest were in bed, I laid down for my few hours of rest.

I jumped up in a blind rush when I heard the alarm clock. I hurried to get cereal and coffee ready and managed to get Will and the hunters out the door in record time. Once we were at our listening spot deep in the woods, we all sat down and waited. Minutes passed and finally Will spoke. "Man it's dark this morning".

A few more minutes passed and Will spoke again. "Cuz what

time is it?"

I looked at my watch and it read exactly 1:30 a.m. Some how I must have dreamed the clock went off and never really checked the time before heading out. Neither Will nor our guest were amused by the early morning hike.

On the last day of the 1987 season, I was too excited to be tired. I was scheduled for a week's vacation after the final hunt and had only one last day before some serious rest and relaxation. I was hunting with Jimmy Primos near Rolling Fork, Mississippi. Jimmy and I didn't hear anything at daybreak and pulled another marathon hike that raised one gobble. We said our good-byes at noon and I headed my truck south. I stopped and called my wife and told hear that I would be home around 3 p.m. I suggested we go out and celebrate a successful and, more importantly, completed turkey season.

Her reply was "I'd love to. Do you think you can stay awake during dinner?"

After about an hour on the road, I felt myself starting to nod a bit. I found a place on the side of the road and pulled over to rest my eyes for a minute. I had plenty of time and knew I would be better rested when I arrived home for my night on the town with Pam.

I parked my truck in a shady spot off of Highway 61 and pulled my cap down over my eyes. The next sound I heard was a sharp rap on my window. I opened my eyes to see a Mississippi State Trooper holding a flashlight and motioning me to roll my window down.

He asked me if I was all right and if there was a problem. I assured him I was just resting and he smiled and turned to walk off. I sat up and grabbed the wheel, and just as it hit me that it was dark outside, the trooper stepped back to my window and said, "By the way, you need to call your wife. She's worried about you."

I looked at my watch and it was 7 p.m. My little nap turned into five hours. To say my wife was upset would be mild.

Since that season, I have learned to pace myself a bit better and never try to drive when I'm tired. I also make sure that when I ask the blessing, I end it with a silent request that the Lord never let me fall asleep at the dinner table again. One of the most blatant cases of pure sleep deprivation I ever witnessed was on a turkey hunt in Texas. Now Texas is a bit different when it comes to hunting turkeys.

When you're in the outdoor industry and part of your job is to entertain customers, outdoor writers and the like, you enjoy Texas because of the shear number of turkeys. You can get almost anyone a turkey in Texas. The problem is sunrise is about 6:30 a.m. and turkeys go to roost about 8:30 p.m. That can make for a long day.

When you are on an extended visit, say 10 days or so, a good night's rest is rare. Invited guests are fresh when they arrive and want to stay up talking about turkeys and then hunt all day. When you have three or four groups in over a two-week stretch, then you learn all about sleep deprivation. On one particular hunt I was part of a group that was guiding some outdoor writers. I had left my video camera in camp and taken a new cameraman along to video the hunt.

The cameraman was new and I thought I would give him some camera tips during the hunt. Keep in mind, this new camera-man had been with us for eight straight days and was not use to such a blistering schedule. As luck would have it, we hooked up with a Rio Grande gobbler around 9 a.m. and followed him for almost two hours. His hens finally gave him the slip and he turned and started moving toward our set up.

This old boy gobbled like an eastern bird and was finally fired up and ready to play the game. I motioned to the cameraman to get ready and relayed the same message to the writer. At 50 yards, the gobbler stopped and drummed so loud you could have heard him in Houston.

He spun and gobbled and really put on a show. I could only imagine how good the video was going to be. Once out of strut, the gobbler moved into gun range and once again posed for the camera. I whispered to the cameraman, "Let us know when you're ready."

No response.

I whispered again, "You ready?"

No response.

By now the gobbler was at about 18 yards and still coming. I cut my eyes toward the cameraman to find his head down and arm propped on the top of the camera. He was out like a light. Just minutes earlier I had made eye contact with him and received a thumbs up. I don't know how he went to sleep so fast with a gobbler sounding off so close, but indeed he had.

I gave the writer the "take him" signal, which he did, and the only one more startled by the blast than the gobbler was the cameraman. To say he came around quickly would be accurate.

Turkey season is about a lot of things: A fresh new look at nature when all is blooming, a strategic battle between hunter and game, a test of patience and skill, but most of all, turkey season is about running on empty.

Gray Hairs and Long Beards

"Slow down son, you'll be flying turkeys out of the trees."

Sixty-three-year-old Fox Haas, of West Point, Mississippi, snapped a gentle command to remind me to slow my pace as we headed down the logging road in the pre-dawn darkness. Never mind if it was Mr. Fox's first trip to Missouri and he was not accustomed to the steep terrain, he knew his game plan long before we ever left camp.

Mr. Fox pulled out a single sheet of paper that contained a pencil sketch of the area. He held his glasses with one hand up to his eyes and studied the map by the glow of my flashlight.

"I think we can listen from here if its good by you Cuz."

"Yes sir, Mr. Fox, that's good by me," I replied.

I felt as though I was with Vince Lombardi and he was about to take me under his wing and teach me how to coach the Packers through the first Super Bowl.

I took the heavy video camera and tripod off my shoulder and set it down in the road. I tried to concentrate on the still sounds of the woods in hopes of hearing the first gobble of the morning. The silence was broken by the sound of Mr. Fox pouring coffee from his thermos.

"Relax and have a shot," he whispered.

I declined the java and sat down next to Mr. Fox and resigned myself to slowing down and just enjoying the morning. Somewhere around the second sip of coffee, a gobbler sounded off to the south. I stood up and shouldered the video gear and took a few steps in the direction of the gobble.

"Cuz, I'm gonna put a rock in your pants if you don't settle down."

"Yes sir, I just thought we might head that way before it gets good light."

Mr. Fox smiled and sipped his coffee while I paced back and forth waiting for his blessing to head toward the gobbler. Just as the top went back on the thermos, another gobbler sounded off less than two hundred yards from our listening spot. Mr. Fox smiled and spoke, "That one is a bit closer Cuz, let's go set up on him." Enough said.

I followed Mr. Fox until he found a location suitable for his set up. Once he was ready, I adjusted my video camera and pointed it in his direction. Thirty minutes later I watched through the viewfinder as the Missouri gobbler strutted into view and caught the full load of Mr. Fox's No. 6 shot and went down. He walked slowly to the downed gobbler and studied it silently for several minutes.

"These Missouri turkeys sure gobble good. Let's go get a biscuit Cuz."

That spring morning in Missouri was indeed a treat for me. I had known Fox Haas for several years and was excited to get a chance to hunt with him. Fox is the father of Toxey Haas, the inventor of Mossy Oak Camouflage, and it is no wonder Toxey loves the outdoors more than life itself.

Fox Haas has been hunting turkeys since 1947. He is successful each season and has more tales than a snake oil salesman. He grew up hunting turkeys along the Alabama River, and learned to hunt turkeys with life long friend, Neil Fredrick.

"I learned about calling turkeys on a cedar box, but the first gobbler I ever killed I used a mouth call I built myself," he said. "It was made from a piece of heavy copper wire hammered flat with a condom stretched across it. I could make some fair sounds with it, but my first commercial mouth call made by Jim Ratcliff of Mobile, Alabama, sounded really good. I called in many a gobbler with that old call."

Today he hunts much like he did 40 years ago. Patience and a slow pace are traits that many senior turkey hunters share, and he says that back in the early years a slow pace was all he knew.

He says, "When I first started turkey hunting, we would wait for a turkey to gobble and then move to within a safe distance and set up. Back then we would build a blind out of limbs and branches and try to wait an old gobbler out. If he went off another direction gobbling, we would move in that direction and set up with another make shift blind. After a few years of hunting like that, we had blinds all over the woods."

Today Mr. Fox takes advantage of the Mossy Oak camouflage that blends so well in the turkey woods and moves more on gobblers without taking time to build blinds. He does carry a lightweight blind that allows him more movement during those long waits. Another tactic that has changed with age for Haas is locating calls. In the past Haas used only owl hoots and occasional loud yelps to try and get a gobbler to answer. Today he has taken a few pages from son Toxey's book and added cutting to his bag of tricks.

He explains, "Toxey first turned me on to this cuttin' call for locating gobblers. I do it on a mouth call, but it was hard to learn the call. I practiced for a long time to get it sound like Toxey's and have located lots of gobblers in the past few years cuttin'. It's not a call I use while set up working a gobbler, but it will sure provoke a gobble."

I have hunted with Mr. Fox more than once and the soft sounds he produces are pure music. Purrs, clucks, soft yelps and scratching in the leaves are common calls Haas uses when working a gobbler. The amount of calling he does depends on the gobbler and how he is acting. He will increase his calling if he has hens close by that are vocal. He will also hush and wait a gobbler out for hours if he feels it is needed.

The patient hunting method of Fox Haas has resulted in the demise of many old gobblers. One hunt he recalls vividly took place in LA (Lower Alabama) at his favorite hunting spot, Choctaw Bluff.

The Bluff, as most locals call it, has been the hunting land of the Stimpson family of Alabama for many years. The Stimpsons were largely responsible for conservation efforts that resulted in state game laws to protect wildlife in Alabama.

One of Mr. Fox's most memorable hunts took place at The Bluff several years ago on a dreary morning close to the Alabama River. He had heard gobblers fighting in an area two weeks earlier and went back to the area for a late season hunt. Nothing gobbled at daylight, but he decided to set up and wait for a while.

"Around 7:30 a.m. I made a call on my box call and a gobbler answered about three hundred yards away," Mr. Fox said. "My first impulse was to move closer, but I decided to stay put and see what would happen. The gobbler would answer every call but would not move any closer.

"Around 9:30 a.m., a thick fog moved in and I could not see more than fifty yards. The gobbler shut up for a long time, so I just waited. I heard him gobble once about 10:30 and once more about twenty minutes later. I decided to call and this time the gobbler went nuts.

"He gobbled 40 or 50 times in the next 15 minutes. At about 11:45 he stepped out of the fog at 35 yards. After a four-hour wait, I shot the twenty-pound gobbler at twenty-five yards. It was a great hunt. Looking back, I feel if I had tried to move on the gobbler I would not have gotten him."

Mr. Fox's patient hunting method comes from years of experience. Today he may cover more ground than in the past, but he still will set up and wait out even the toughest gobblers. He feels that is his best tactic.

Another seasoned hunter who shares many of Mr. Fox's slow hunting tactics is 59- year-old Jack Bellas of Estill, South Carolina. Jack has been turkey hunting for 33 years, the last eight of those with a video camera.

Jack now guides hunters for turkeys and whitetails at the Tri-County Hunting Lodge in Estill. Jack sees all types of hunters through his guiding services and believes many of today's hunters hunt too fast while pursuing spring gobblers.

According to Jack, "Patience is the key when hunting gobblers. Many hunters today concentrate on their calling skills much more than good woodsmanship. I can understand anyone wanting to find a gobbling turkey, but many days that is not going to happen. I spend time every day in the woods and learn where turkeys are. I learn where they roost and feed and spend time during the day.

"Many times I will take hunters to places knowing turkeys will be there sooner or later. Often the hunters do not want to wait them out. They would rather cover ground and call to get a response from a gobbler. If a gobbler has hens with him he may not gobble at all during the day. That is when knowing the land and where the turkeys are, certainly is a big plus."

Jack learned his patient methods in the days when gobblers were not abundant in the South Carolina. He would hunt for days without hearing or seeing a turkey. Once he found turkeys, he would stay with them until one of them won the game.

He continues, "Back when turkeys were hard to find, I would cover lots of ground to find a flock. Once I located the birds, I would stay with them. I might sit for the better part of a day in one spot and call very little.

"Most often if you located turkeys, there would be lots of

hens, so calling was not always the key. I would have to get in close to the turkeys and be there when they flew down to try and get a gobbler. Today, turkeys are much more abundant, and even though they are easier to find, I still believe good woodsmanship and knowing where the turkeys are and what they do during the day is most important when hunting."

Jack started out his turkey-hunting career using a Lynch box call. He still carries that box call today, but uses mostly a mouth call when hunting.

He says, "I use mainly a mouth call now because it frees my hands up to operate my video camera. I also am able to make better soft calls like whines and purrs on the mouth call. These soft calls are very important when working turkeys in close. Louder yelps and cuts are fine when trying to locate gobblers, but I find I have the most luck imitating the soft sounds hens make while feeding in the woods."

The slow hunting patient hunting tactics of Jack and Fox Haas came to my attention in a big way during the spring of '93. Most southern hunters will remember that spring as the one that brought us the "Storm of the Century." With 20 inches of snow on the ground in Birmingham, Alabama, Fox Haas, son Toxey and I headed to South Carolina to open the early South Carolina spring season. What is usually a 12-hour drive took almost 16 due to the snow. We arrived at the Tri-County Hunting Lodge during the night and were less than enthusiastic about our chances for opening morning.

Jack awakened us the next morning. He stood on the porch with pipe in hand and spoke, "Wear some warm clothes boys, its pretty cold out here today."

The mercury was hanging around 28 degrees as Toxey and I drove away from the Tri-State Lodge. Jack and Fox were still at the camp when we left and seemed in no hurry to open the season.

Toxey and I had a hard time hearing a gobbler that morning. Jack assured us that gobblers were in the area he sent us, but I believe the cold weather had their gobble boxes frozen. Toxey and I were back at camp around 9:30 but there was no sign of Jack and Fox.

Eventually, Jack's old brown pick-up pulled into the camp and the two gray hairs stepped out grinning from ear to ear. Bellas reached into one side of the truck and pulled out his video camera while Haas reached into the other side and pulled out a big Carolina gobbler.

Jack and Mr. Fox had not heard any gobblers that morning, but Jack had scouted well and knew where turkeys were roosted and would most likely be after fly down.

Mr. Fox told us that Jack hunted at the same pace he was accustomed to, and he and Jack were really in sync all morning.

Mr. Fox continues, "Jack and I went into the area and sipped coffee while we waited for a gobbler to sound off. Nothing gobbled, so we just headed into the woods and set up where Jack felt would be a good spot. We finally heard a gobbler at about 8:30. Jack motioned to me to make a few calls. I yelped softly a few times and then shut up.

"We finally saw the turkeys through the brush. There were several turkeys and one full strutting gobbler. We made no more calls and the turkeys moved very little for what seemed like an hour. Finally, the turkeys made their way toward us. At one point we had several hens within a few feet. The Mossy Oak camouflage did its job and, before long, the strutting gobbler moved in for a 20 yard shot."

Jack and Mr. Fox had waited on the turkeys for more than four hours. Their patience had paid off with not only a fine South Carolina gobbler, but a new friendship as well. Over the next few days, Jack and Mr. Fox hunted together and treated us to many gobbler stories at night.

There is a lot to be said for the slow paced, laid-back hunting styles of these two veterans. Taking your time and knowing the land is a big advantage in anyone's book. Jack and Mr. Fox indeed take their time when hunting spring gobblers, but never lose sight of what is most important.

Mr. Fox summed it up well when he told us his feelings about turkey hunting.

"I hunt the way I hunt because I enjoy that style. If someone else chooses a different pace or style that's fine. I say do what makes you happy and just be safe."

Mossy Oak Moments

I dared not blink while the poacher scanned the ridge for the source of the turkey sounds he had undoubtedly heard coming from my slate moments earlier. The scope on top of the .22 magnum looked ominous through the lens of my video camera, which was zoomed to 14 power. I managed to push the record button and capture the stealth moves of the trespasser as he worked his way closer to my set up.

It was obvious that this person was not looking for a gobbler to harvest, so any movement on my part could have been disastrous. I tried not to breathe as the poacher passed within 15 yards of me, still looking for his target. Once past my location, the intruder scanned the open field with his riflescope and then disappeared from view.

When I set up that afternoon on a ridge leading to a large clover field, I had no idea I would call up anything other than the turkeys that had been using that field every day. I was hunting just north of Natchez, Mississippi on land upon which I had permission to film turkeys. The poacher could not believe it when the sheriff showed him the videotape of him sneaking through the woods with his rifle raised on the posted land. The landowner remarked to the poacher that he had those surveillance cameras all over the woods, so don't try sneaking around on that property anymore.

I have been in many situations afield that tested the limits of good camouflage. That afternoon was, without a doubt, the most intense test I have ever endured.

Looking back, I probably should have shouted at the poacher from a distance, but I decided to video him instead. Once I saw the intense look on his face and his finger on the trigger of his rifle, I decided to just let him pass. I had no idea he would walk within a few feet of my set up.

I learned two things that day. One was to never think turkeys

To this day, Toxey Haas will tell you he invented Mossy Oak to help fool the eyes of the wild turkey. When it comes to hunting, Toxey is the real deal.

are the only things listening to your calling. The other was that Mossy Oak camouflage would always be the pattern I wore in the field. To this day, the poacher had no idea I was sitting against a pine tree with 80 pounds and several thousand dollars worth of commercial video gear in my lap.

That was back in 1987 while I was working for Will Primos. Shortly after seeing Will in his Mossy Oak, I had my own outfit and also had covered all my video equipment with Mossy Oak tape. Camera, tripod, recording decks and microphones all blended into the woods like dirt. The only attention that video camera ever raised was when I strolled into one of my daughter's dance recitals with it over my shoulder. My wife was not impressed with the great camo job I had done on the video gear.

Toxey Haas, the inventor of the Mossy Oak pattern, has spent his share of time in the woods in pursuit of turkeys as well. One only has to spend a short amount of time with Toxey to realize that no other person on the planet is more devoted to hunting, especially turkey hunting, than he is. These days, Toxey is also focused on conservation and passing on the hunting tradition. Mossy Oak was in Toxey's head years before he developed the pattern. He confessed to me that even while hunting turkeys as a kid with his dad, he used to dream of being invisible to game. That thought stuck with Toxey through the years and even while in college he never lost sight of his dream, to design the perfect camouflage. Toxey had to learn as he ran with the Mossy Oak idea. He knew nothing about the fabric business, but knew what he wanted in a camouflage. Many suppliers told him that his idea would not fly, or they could not come up with the colors he wanted. At some point, Toxey put everything together and began sewing the first outfits of Mossy Oak. Once the hunting public saw the product, he was off and running.

Toxey said that Mossy Oak has been successful for one reason, and that's effectiveness. The fact that Mossy Oak works for hunters has made it the leader in the camouflage industry.

Having known Toxey for years, I can understand what he means when he says hunters have made Mossy Oak successful. He has always listened to hunters and their needs. He hunts regularly and knows first hand how to make clothes for people who depend on their camouflage.

Toxey learned his hunting skills from his father, Fox Haas, who taught him early on how to enjoy and respect wildlife.

According to Toxey, "Of all the things my father passed on to me, the ability to judge people has been my most valued asset. Sure, I had a passion for the outdoors and worked hard to develop great camo patterns, but the people that I have around me are what have made Mossy Oak."

You don't have to spend much time inside the loop at Mossy Oak to see that people are the driving force. People who are focused, enthused, busy and, most of all, happy. The atmosphere around the office is unlike any corporate environment you'll encounter any place else. During spring months, you're likely to find a deceased wild turkey gobbler hanging near the rear entrance to Mossy Oak, Inc.

My first turkey hunt with Toxey took place near my home in the spring of 1987.

Once again we were trying to video a successful spring hunt. I was running the camera and Haas was going to call and, hopefully, shoot a long beard on video.

Our hunt started out slowly to say the least. No gobbles at daylight are bad news when you're carrying 80 pounds of video gear. It means walking and covering ground until you get some action. I handed the 30-pound tripod to Toxey and we took off walking, stopping to call every few hundred yards.

About 45 minutes and a mile or so later, Haas blew his crow call and we heard a faint gobble. We did the normal arguing about which direction the sound came from and decided we needed another gobble to be sure. This time I backed off about 40 yards while Haas blew the crow call once more. This time we both pointed in the same direction and headed into the woods in the direction of the faint gobble.

A few hundred yards into the woods, we were looking at a wide-open swamp that had little or no cover to move around in. We decided to stop and set up and not chance spooking the gobbler. Toxey sat down against a tree with his back to me and I backed off about 25 yards behind him. I had some cover and wasted no time getting the camera ready to capture Toxey's first call. I looked through the viewfinder to focus on Toxey but he was nowhere to be found. I scanned the area where I watched him sit down, but still no Toxey. Finally he let out a soft yelp and I found him.

He had moved a few feet from where he had originally sat down. He had literally disappeared in a small bush he found to his right.

A few more soft yelps from Haas got no response from the gobbler. I was convinced the turkey had gone in another direction. Just as I was about to signal Toxey from my set up he slowly began to move his gun. I caught movement to my right and there was the gobbler. He had come in totally silent and was looking right in our direction. Haas had already managed to get his gun on the gobbler and was waiting for my signal to shoot. I found the red head in my viewfinder and gave a soft cluck to Toxey, which was the signal to shoot. At the gun blast, the gobbler folded and flopped for only a second.

While I interviewed Toxey with video camera rolling, he never mentioned the effectiveness of his Mossy Oak.

He talked about his dad, turkeys, and how one day he would be taking his kids along on something he loved so much. Talking about turkeys and the outdoors came as natural to him as calling turkeys.

Seeing first-hand how much Toxey loves turkey hunting, its no wonder he came up with such an effective pattern. Toxey spends countless hours in the field and is always looking for ways to improve his hunting techniques. Camouflage is much more to him than clothing; it is a tool that he depends on in the field. I can promise you that in 1986 when Toxey was perfecting the original Mossy Oak Bottomland pattern, he was not thinking about marketing strategy or consumer shares. His thoughts were on hunting and effective camouflage. To say he was a man possessed with a passion would be at the very least correct.

Today Mossy Oak is a well-known and instantly recognizable brand to millions of consumers. In 1988, I went to work for Toxey and, for the next several years, I wore many hats so to speak. Sales, public relations and, finally, back in the video production side of the business.

In 1996, Mossy Oak launched its first national television program, "Hunting the Country." I had the task of producing that program and, along with a very talented team of people, watched it grow to become the highest-rated outdoor cable program in the nation. Breaking into the television business is no easy task. Our team was basically hunters whose love of the outdoors was motivation enough to learn the broadcast business. I can only smile when I think back to the days where we were just walking the woods with no plan, no script and no idea about commercial broadcast needs. What we had was a little hunting savvy, a love of the outdoors and lots of desire.

Calling Too Much and Too Loud

There are many phrases one hears during a lifetime that stick in the mind.

"Give me liberty or give me death."

"I regret that I have but one life to give for my country."

"An apple a day keeps the doctor away."

And one of my all time favorites: "Where's the beef?"

For most people, for whatever reason, there always seems to be one quote that is close at hand. It may be an inspirational term that keeps them motivated. For instance, "Early to bed and early to rise makes a man healthy, wealthy and wise." Maybe it's "A penny saved is a penny earned," or "The longest journey begins with one step." I have heard all those famous phrases and think of them and many others from time to time.

The one statement I hear in my mind more than any, though, is, "You call too much and you call too loud." Man if had a dollar every time I've heard that I'd be rich.

The calling too much and too loud terminology as it relates to turkey hunting has probably been around as long as turkey hunting itself. I can picture two Indians hidden with bow and arrow, set up and calling to a flock of turkeys. One of the native hunters is older and more experienced; the other is young and not so polished. The young one has a blade of grass between his thumbs making his best imitation of a yelp and is calling away at a strutting gobbler. All of a sudden, the older Indian pulls an arrow from his quiver and pops his student on the leg. The older Indian then puts his finger to his mouth as to say, "Hey buddy, you're calling too much and too loud."

If you learned your turkey hunting skills from an older, more experienced hunter, then the same thing has happened to you. Maybe you didn't get smacked on the leg with an arrow, but the message has been delivered in one form or another since people hunted turkeys.

The way people call and hunt turkeys has always been somewhat of a fascination to me. I have had the privilege of going along with literally hundreds of people. Many were well known, some were legends in the sport and many others were just great hunters. I have hunted with professional callers that have won world, national, regional and state titles. Some of the modern day callers sound better than real live hens. The talent these people have and the sounds they produce are unbelievable. Some of them are much better callers than they are hunters. Some have the deadly combination of being both.

One thing that is constant with most great turkey callers and hunters is they believe their method and their hunting technique is the best. Success in the turkey woods brings confidence. Each and every hunter who kills turkeys sometimes thinks his attack plan is the total and final formula to turkey hunting success. It doesn't take hundreds of killing shots to make a turkey hunter feel he has this game figured out. Many hunters feel they have reached the pinnacle after two or three kills. I myself may have been guilty of thinking this way early on.

To this day when I am hunting with someone for the first time, I find myself trying to run the hunt, so to speak. Reverting to my own personal style just seems to creep into the hunt. This has been shaped by several circumstances that literally forced me to do things in a certain way.

Like most turkey hunters, I learned from people who had been doing it for years before I entered the sport. I learned early on that you call very little, never call before the gobbler flies down and then only two or three soft yelps every 10 or 15 minutes. This method works well for many set ups, but if there is one thing that is true about hunting turkeys, it is there are NO absolutes. I repeat, there are NO absolutes. This point is proven to me time and time again by the turkeys themselves.

In the late 1980s, I went hunting with a fellow who was a world-class caller. This fellow was a very experienced contest caller and had recently won the world turkey-calling contest. I was going to try to video the champ bagging a gobbler and was pretty excited about the hunt. It was late in the season and, down South, the late April foliage, heat and humidity can make all-day hunts a challenge. I was hoping the champ could call one in quickly and the rest of the morning could be spent shooting interviews.

I walked outside at 5 a.m. and was greeted by a brilliant star-filled sky, no wind, and a surprisingly cool morning for south Mississippi. Things were looking great.

I met the champ at the local quick shop and headed to my listening point. As soon as we stepped out of the truck, we heard a gobble. Usually when a turkey is sounding off in the pitch dark, it's a really good sign he is lonesome. A few minutes and several gobbles later we were set up. I was just behind the champ and had my video camera ready to roll.

I was not about to pull any of my calls out since the champ was going to do all the calling. My calling is more than adequate, but world-class it ain't. The gobbler continued to sound off and I heard no hen sounds nearby. I was convinced this old boy was alone in the woods and this hunt might be over fast.

For fifteen minutes I waited for the champ to call. He didn't make a sound. The gobbler was choking himself and still not even a soft tree call from the champ. Just as I thought the champ was about to make his first call, a lone hen cackled and flew down 100 yards to the west.

The gobbler doubled gobbled and pitched straight to the hen. The hen led the gobbler off into the timber and our hunt was over without so much as a cluck from the champ. This is one case where a few calls from the hunter might have brought the gobbler straight in. Just because the rules say don't call much when the gobbler is in the tree doesn't mean there isn't a situation that demands it.

In 1986, I went to work for a game call company, which at the time was just getting up and running. The company was in the process of trying to make a turkey hunting video and knew that I was doing some amateur video work.

Long story short, we hooked up and began trying to teach ourselves how to use this huge TV camera in the woods and hide it from turkeys. During this process is when I began to call much more aggressively than in the past. I would hunt all day, and the best way I found to record hunts was to locate gobbling turkeys. Although the most comfortable way to handle the camera was to set up in one spot, call and wait, it was not as productive as finding gobblers that were ready to be movie stars.

The act of covering ground and calling was basically where

my reputation for calling too much and too loud came from. Most of the hunters who tagged along on these video hunts all seemed to have the same comment. I would call loudly when trying to locate.

If the turkeys were coming in, I would continue to call aggressively for two reasons. One, it was to get more gobbling on videotape, and two, it was to try and close the deal before something went wrong. Many times, technical problems would arise: Dead batteries, running out of tape, microphones going dead and so on. I figured out that the sooner the gobbler came in and got shot, the better my chances for getting it all on camera would be. Once that first video was completed, the response from the turkey-hunting public was huge. People loved the great hunting action, the misses and interaction between hunters.

After the video had been on the market for a while, I started hearing comments about calling too much and calling too loud. One instance stands out, which occurred at a sporting goods store where I was doing a seminar using some of the spring footage for visual aid. One hunt I showed the crowd was a quick hunt that had lots of calling and gobbling. The turkey was a two-year-old that was gobbling at any sound I made. I called a lot and the gobbler responded with booming gobbles in mid-stride.

The turkey was shot at 20 yards and the hunt took only three or four minutes. When the video was turned off, an older gentleman stood up and shook his finger and said, "You call too much and too loud. You can't kill turkeys like that." Never mind we just showed him UN-edited videotape of the hunt; this guy was upset that we had the nerve to claim we did that.

True enough, most turkeys will not tolerate a lot of excited calling. If they are hunted a lot and are used to getting spooked, then quiet, subtle calls and patience are usually the key.

I still hunt that way most of the time, but if the turkey likes the calling, and if I'm not worried about other hunters coming in, and if I am trying to get footage of gobbling and strutting, then I'll call a lot. This doesn't mean that I blow his feathers off at 20 yards with a tube call. Like most other turkey hunters, I will adjust my calling to the situation.

It's knowing how to differentiate the situations that make calling a lot or a little work. One aspect of turkey hunting that does require calling a lot and loudly is locating. I firmly believe people routinely walk by most of their huntable turkeys because they don't make them gobble. If you're walking the woods and calling or prospecting, then volume is a plus. In my humble opinion, a turkey is listening to subtle turkey sounds all day. Another soft yelp is probably not going to provoke a gobble. I prefer a sharp, loud cutt or a loud yelp for locating. Whether it's a box call, slate, diaphragm or my favorite, a tube call, find something that generates volume for reaching out long distances. When you're trying to cover lots of ground and pull a gobble from a reluctant tom, feel free to call too much and too loud. Once you've got a response and sit down to try and call the gobbler up, then adjust to the situation. Most often this will mean calling just enough to let the gobbler know you're there.

If you get no response in a lengthy amount of time, then try another loud, sharp call. Knowing when to do this just comes with experience. Many times a gobbler will shock gobble at a loud cutt when he has hens already with him. Even if he has no intention of coming in, at least you'll know where he is. Deciding when to move and how to hunt the gobbler then becomes the challenge.

There are also times when calling aggressively doesn't hurt a thing. If you're set up at daylight on a gobbler and hens are yelping and clucking loudly in the trees all around, then you better get your name in the hat. You may convince the hens to fly down in your direction. If that happens, then the gobbler may follow. In this case, soft calling is pointless.

Another time when calling loud is demanded is on extremely windy days. With a brisk, 20-plus mile-per-hour wind, you better generate all the volume you can muster. When it's very windy, you should double everything. Cover twice as much ground; call twice as loud and twice as often. Turkeys are still turkeys, even after a cold front has brought freezing temps and high wind.

The knack of knowing when to call softly and when to crank it out will come with experience. Spending countless days in the turkey woods will teach you what to do and when to do it. There will always be many factors to consider.

Here are a couple of different scenarios and what I would do:

You are walking and calling around mid-morning and you raise a gobble from about 300 yards. You decide to close the distance just a bit before setting up. You move toward the gobble and discover a small creek.

The creek is several feet deep and full of water. The gobbler is gobbling and heading in your direction and there is no way you can cross the creek without spooking the gobbler. What do you do? Option one: I would first set up and hide really well, as this plan may take a while. If the gobbler shows and is indeed alone and you need him to fly the creek to be in gun range, I would continue to call softly and see if he would fly the creek. He is probably going to strut and gobble a while and then walk off.

If you see this happening, then crank it up and try and get him so excited that he has to fly the creek. Option two is to let him walk off, cross the creek as quietly as possible and then set up on the other side to try and call him back. If option one works, then you didn't get wet and you got your gobbler. If option one fails, then I guarantee you that gobbler will still be thinking about you when you get across the creek and start your calling again.

Scenario two:

You spot a flock of turkeys in an open field. There is one long beard and couple of jakes and a dozen or so hens. You get close to the field and make a few calls. Nothing happens. What to do? I would try to move as close as possible to the flock while paying attention to the direction it's moving. If soft yelps bring no response, then you have nothing to lose. Crank out some excited calls and maybe you can get the jakes to come. Chances are the gobbler might not like the juveniles going to a hen and he'll tag along to crash the party. You just never know.

Bottom line is, don't be scared to call. If your calls sound like turkeys, then most times, you're not going to do any harm. After you have located a gobbler, then most cases will require soft calling and very little of it. On the other hand, and despite what the turkey-hunting gurus might say, there are times when calling too much and too loud will turn the tide.

Turkey Hunting New Zealand

The first gobble echoed in the distance well before daybreak. One of my hunting companions immediately sprang into action.

"I knew there was a mob hanging there mate. Grab your torch and we'll shuffle past the billabong and hear again," he whispered.

My reply was also immediate.

"Say what?"

This time my partner spoke in terms I could understand.

"I knew there was a flock roosting near here, Cuz. Grab your flashlight and we'll sneak down past that pond and listen from there."

This turkey hunt was indeed going to be different. It was taking place in New Zealand and believe me, that is about as far from Mississippi as you can get.

As we made our way through the darkness near the billabong (pond), turkeys were gobbling with each step. Toxey Haas of Mossy Oak camouflage, the third member of our party, stopped Mark Draper, our Kiwi guide, and suggested we set up near a small opening and not risk getting any closer. Soon Toxey was set up calling to the gobblers while Mark and I watched from a few yards back.

I strained through the viewfinder of my video camera to see any movement from the line of trees where the birds were roosted. The early dawn light soon revealed a full fan against the morning sky. I panned the camera above the one gobbler to discover five more Toms strutting on one limb. For the next 10 minutes, we watched and listened as the turkeys made every sound in their vocabulary. Yelps, clucks, purrs, gobbles. If these turkeys were any different from the ones we hunted in the States, it wasn't apparent in the sounds they made.

The first turkey out of the tree was a hen. She hit the ground and began yelping loudly while moving away from our set up. Before long, every turkey in the roost pitched toward the loud mouth hen and began feeding slowly behind her. Toxey motioned to me that we should get up and move to get in front of the flock. I followed his moves with camera in hand and in less than 10 minutes, Toxey's calling from our second location had two strutting gobblers and several hens in gun range. The gun bucked and our first close up look at a New Zealand gobbler was at hand.

The 20-pound Kiwi gobbler looked very similar to the Merriam turkeys found in the western United States. On this hunt, the sounds and tactics were similar to turkey hunting in the States, but over the next nine days, we would realize some of the differences between chasing gobblers in the lower 48 and chasing them down under.

My New Zealand hunt began two years ago while at an Outdoor Writers convention in Portland, Oregon. Jim Grassi, of the California-based Rod and Reel Adventures Travel Service, approached me after viewing some of the Primos' "Truth About Turkey Hunting" videos, which I had a hand in filming and editing. He knew that I was a turkey hunter and might be interested in hearing about all these turkeys in New Zealand, that had virtually no pressure from hunters or predators.

Grassi had been guiding fishermen in New Zealand for quite a while and had seen first-hand the large numbers of turkeys that inhabited both the North and South Island.

After visiting with Grassi and viewing some of the photos of not only the turkeys but the country as well, I began to strategize how I could make it happen. Enter Toxey Haas.

Toxey is the inventor of Mossy Oak camouflage and, more importantly, my boss. He is also one of the nation's best and most enthusiastic turkey hunters. His love of this sport was the driving force behind the birth of Mossy Oak camouflage, and although he pursues many types of big game, turkeys have always remained his first love when it comes to hunting. My next step was to get Grassi and Toxey Haas together, with our wives, for a business meeting. Once the wives got wind of the possibilities of a trip to New Zealand, it didn't take long for rock solid plans to emerge.

Our New Zealand trip was scheduled for early September and would take place on the North Island. Jim Grassi told us to save the South Island for our second visit because no one comes to New Zealand only once. September is early spring down under and was much like early March or late February in the southern United States.

I did as much research as possible ahead of time to see what problems, if any, I would have trying to video the trip. The electrical current is 230 instead of 110, so I secured proper adapters for battery chargers and other electrical items and readied cameras and camouflage for my second spring of 1994.

The flight from Los Angeles to Auckland, New Zealand, lasted more than 12 hours. All Air New Zealand flights leave in the evening from L.A. and most people manage to sleep for most of the flight. I was not so lucky and was glad to finally see the sun coming up over the North Island when our plane touched down. Another short flight transported our crew from Auckland to Whakatane near the Bay of Plenty where Mark Draper met us.

Mark operates a professional guiding service that includes hunts for red stag, ducks and other big game and some of the best fly-fishing in the world. Mark prefers a house stay for his hunting clients. Our party enjoyed the stay with Mark and Diane in their home. The accommodations, the food and general feeling of being truly welcome made us all more than comfortable.

Although Mark was a seasoned guide, he admitted that he was a bit new to this turkey hunting game, but had done some homework and was excited about the possibilities of more turkey hunters from the States visiting his country. Mark, Toxey and I talked at length about terrain, strategies and what we might expect from these Kiwi gobblers.

Our first hunt as described earlier was typical and delightful. I was able to capture the whole event on videotape and felt like this was going to be all that I bargained for.

Our first afternoon hunt really opened my eyes. We pulled up on a hilltop where our view was breathtaking. The lush, green, rolling terrain looked as though it had been hand painted to impress the tourists. Mark, Toxey and I went only a few hundred yards when Mark kneeled down and whispered to Toxey, "Give that call a toot, mate." Toxey yelped and several gobblers answered. From that moment on, I began to learn what much of this New Zealand turkey hunting would be like.

We spotted the flock, or mob, as the Kiwis call them, from several hundred yards away. This flock had five strutting, mature gobblers, seven hens, and three juvenile gobblers or jakes. The flock seemed to stay close together while they fed on the lush grass. Our best calling efforts would not entice the gobblers away from the hens. For the next hour, we called and the gobblers would respond by strutting and gobbling. At times, two of the gobblers would respond by strutting and gobbling. Occasionally, two of the gobblers would move in our direction, but would only travel a few yards and return to the flock.

The open, rolling terrain made it hard to move without being spotted. Eventually the turkeys fed into an area that enabled us to pick up and move in order to get closer and in front of the flock. Even though we had limited or no cover, the Mossy Oak Full Foliage camouflage blended perfectly with the New Zealand landscape. Once we were set up again, Toxey and I both called and once more we received immediate responses from the gobblers.

This time the two longbeards that had been threatening to peel off from the group did exactly that. Toxey waited for the two gobblers to separate and took his shot. This New Zealand gobbler sported a 7-inch beard and weighed 20 pounds. It had taken almost two hours from the time we heard these turkeys to make the shot. For the entire two hours we had the gobblers in full view and watched and listened as they continuously strutted and gobbled. It was quite a show and a bit nerve wracking to have so many turkeys that close for such a long period of time without being able to move.

For the next three days, Mark Draper showed us many locations near the Bay of Plenty that held turkeys. All of the farmers in this area were receptive to turkey hunting on their property, but were not sure what to think about the idea. Until recently, New Zealanders did not consider their turkeys a game bird.

Hunting is a long-standing, respected tradition in New Zealand, but until the recent interest shown from American sportsmen, Kiwi turkeys were passed up in lieu of ducks, pheasants, hogs, and several species of deer including red stag, which is the coveted big game trophy of New Zealand. After three days with Mark Draper and his home stay, we were a bit reluctant to leave his area for the second stage of our New Zealand hunt. Mark transported our group three hours south to Rotorura. Here we were met by Colin Jones and Sue Jolly of Chris Jolly's guide service. Sue Jolly took our wives away for three days of activities that did not include turkey hunting. Colin Jones loaded our gear into his Landrover and headed east.

Colin Jones would prove to be not only a skilled hunter with more than 40 years of hunting experience, but quite a character to boot. When Colin spoke of hunting experience, he had the credentials to back that statement up. The New Zealand government had employed him as a professional hunter for many years. Many of these hunters were needed to keep the deer populations in check. Colin had also guided hundreds of sportsmen for waterfowl hunting and trout fishing. Like Mark Draper, Colin was new to this turkey hunting game but had also done some research into how Americans prefer to hunt turkeys.

One thing the hunting guides shared in New Zealand was their attitude. These were the most professional and dedicated people I have ever been around. They were extremely proud of what they did for a living and put as much effort and training into their livelihood as any doctor, lawyer or other professional person might commit to his career.

After a two-hour drive that took us through some of the most breathtaking countryside imaginable, we arrived in the small town of Te Kuiti. We checked into a small motel and quickly changed back into our Mossy Oak and headed to one of the nearby farms that, according to Colin, held lots of turkeys.

It didn't take long to find turkeys once we arrived at the first farm. Again, we spotted the turkeys with binoculars and moved in closer to try to call them in. I followed closely behind Toxey, who had spotted a beautiful gobbler that was a bronze color with white tipped wings. Toxey set up about 200 yards from the bronze gobbler and began to call. The gobbler instantly answered and began to strut in our direction. I was again filming over Toxey's shoulder and could not believe our good fortune in locating such a beautiful bronze gobbler.

For half an hour the gobbler strutted and gobbled, all the time bringing in more hens to his strutting spot. Toxey whispered to me he was going to move to some nearby trees that he felt the flock would move toward to roost, since it was getting near fly up time. I continued to film as Toxey made his way above the turkeys. Once he was in his new position, he again began to call. This time his calling was a bit more excited and fast paced. Two of the hens began walking straight toward Toxey and the big bronze gobbler followed. Just as light was fading, Toxey's gun roared and the bronze gobbler went down. This gobbler was destined for the taxidermist. He sported a 10-inch beard; one-inch spurs and weighed 21 pounds. It was truly an amazing gobbler that was taken in the middle of some dazzling scenery.

It was clear that Colin Jones had done his homework on lining up private farms that held lots of turkeys. The second day out with Colin, Toxey and I both hunted with archery gear and both managed to bag nice gobblers. Bowhunting these turkeys was great fun. The terrain was perfect for spotting and stalking into a position that allowed us to call the gobblers that last few yards. Even with these virtually unhunted birds, bowhunting them proved to be challenging. It took several tries to get in close enough for good bow shots. The advantage of bowhunting gobblers in New Zealand is the chances at close encounters and bowshots are going to be frequent.

Since the turkeys have no natural predators in New Zealand, their numbers have steadily grown, so much so that today many sheep ranchers consider them a nuisance. According to one of the sheep ranchers we met, six turkeys will eat as much grass as one sheep. That is why the landowners were very receptive to turkey hunting.

The thought of thinning down the large numbers of turkeys and increasing their farm income made for open arms from the farmers, at least the ones we encountered. On each farm we visited, Colin would make sure that along with a portion of the hunting fee we paid, the landowner also received a fillet of smoked trout and a bottle of wine. Watching the guides secure permission to hunt the farms was always a high point for me. It was done with polite conversation and total respect for the land, the landowner and the game.

Our last two days in New Zealand were spent out of the bush. We caught up with our wives at Lake Taupo where Chris and Sue Jolly had treated them to snow skiing, sight seeing, trout fishing and a helicopter ride. Needless to say, they too had experienced the trip of a lifetime.

I left New Zealand with the feeling that I would surely return some day. I had a total respect for the country and most of all, the people. I had met some wonderful people that would remain friends for life. What more could you ask for in a hunting adventure?

Back in Mississippi, Bubba Bruce, one of my long time turkey hunting buddies, asked me, "Cuz, tell me about hunting those turkeys in New Zealand."

After long thought, my reply was, "Bubba, it was like taking all your best hunting pals and chasing two-year-old gobblers that had never been hunted, and doing it in Jurassic Park."

The First Thirty Minutes

It was a few minutes past five when I reached the top of Clear Creek Hill. I had spent more than a few evenings here each spring listening for a gobbler that might decide to sound off after flying to roost. On a still, calm evening, you could hear for more than a mile in any direction. At 5:10 p.m., a lone gobble to the west got my undivided attention. Over the next 10 minutes, this tom would gobble 11 times on his own.

In some states, gobbling in the afternoon might be the norm. In southwest Mississippi, it is rare. Trying to roost a gobbler in the South is chancy at best. It's sort of like getting your lucky jackpot card punched at the grocery store. You never win the weekly jackpot, but you keep on getting that card punched in the hope that someday you'll get lucky. It's the same with roosting turkeys in south Mississippi. You seldom hear one in the evening, but you keep on going back. Just before dark I hiked to within a few hundred yards of the gobbler and did my best imitation of a cackle. The gobbler immediately double gobbled. I hot footed back to my truck and headed for the Jackson, Mississippi airport.

As luck would have it, I had invited an outdoor writer to Mississippi for a spring gobbler hunt. His 7:45 p.m. arrival in Jackson gave me just enough time to locate a gobbler and still make it to the airport. The writer landed on time and our trip back to Natchez, Mississippi, was full of positive remarks by yours truly. I spent most of my time talking about where our second hunt would take place. After all, the first hunt would be over in a few minutes. It was absolutely in the bag. My biggest concern was making sure we did not oversleep. I set two alarm clocks for insurance and was out like a light. I dreamed about the story this outdoor writer would have for *Field & Stream* or *Sports Afield:* "Turkey hunt with Cuz lasts only two minutes."

The next morning I had my writer friend set up and waiting while it was still pitch black. I was sitting next to him with a grin so big I was sure the gobbler might see my teeth. Knowing this hot-to-trot gobbler was only minutes from his demise was almost more than I could bear.

As the woods began to turn a dull gray, I looked at my watch and wondered when this old boy would sound off. I had decided not to call until he broke the silence. After all, I had picked the perfect spot to set up and a lot of calling wasn't going be necessary. I punched my writer friend and reminded him, "It won't be long now."

One hour and five minutes later my grin was gone and, apparently, so was the gobbler without so much as a cluck to let us know he was ever in the world.

My writer friend was un-impressed with my list of excuses on why this hot gobbler had disappeared. I should have known better than to brag to this high-powered media man. I let my ego and high hopes speak despite past experience and hard earned knowledge telling me, "you never know."

When it comes to hunting gobblers in the spring, the only absolute I speak of now is that there are no absolutes. You can follow some basic rules, but be prepared to throw them out the window at times.

For more than a decade, I have been doing seminars, and the trips have taken me to hundreds of locations across the country. The basic theme of my seminar is, "There are no absolutes." The first segment of my presentation covers what I refer to as the first thirty minutes. This is a crucial time at first light when decisions will be made quickly: where to listen from, where to set up, how close to get, when and what call to make and so on.

There are many things to consider when you're dealing with that first thirty minutes. Without question the biggest obstacle you'll face when trying to call a gobbler off the roost is a hen.

Almost all turkey hunts begin at dawn when the gobbler sounds off from his roost. The time between that first gobble and when the gobbler actually flies down can vary, but in most cases, is only a few minutes. Knowing where to set up is crucial. If you've scouted the area and know the turkey's routine, then you may have an idea where to start your hunt. If you've done your homework and have a good idea where the turkey is headed after the fly down, then your hunt may be a short one.

One of the most common questions asked by new turkey hunters is, how close should I get when setting up to call a turkey on the roost? The answer to that is simple: As close as you can without spooking the turkey. What sounds simple is actually complicated. First, you have to know the terrain. Are there any obstacles that could stop the gobbler's progress to you? Creeks, fences even thick cover can stop a gobbler dead in his tracks. You also need to determine how quietly you can make your approach. If you're walking in dry leaves, then you can't get very close. If the woods are damp and the foliage is heavy, you can get closer. If it's early in the year when limbs are bare, naturally the gobbler can see much better. In this condition, you'll need to set up much farther from him.

Another thing to remember is that in heavy foliage, the sound of the gobble will not carry as far. It's very easy to spook a gobbler off the roost under this condition, so take your time when moving in. It's also a good idea to listen to more than one gobble if possible. If the gobbler is facing away from you, he will sound much farther away than when he's facing in your direction. You also need to realize that other turkeys are probably roosted nearby. The gobbler sounding off is very seldom the only turkey roosted in that area. The good rule of thumb is to err on the conservative side. You can always let the morning unfold and move as you need to.

Most turkey hunters will tell you that calling to a gobbler while he's still in the tree is one of those things you should absolutely not do. In some cases, this is good advice. The thinking here is if a gobbler is sounding off loudly and often, then he may actually call up hens or even another hunter. This is often the case and either of the two will usually spoil your hunt. If you're hunting an area you share with other hunters, then you don't want to have them walk into your setup. If this is the case, then try a soft yelp or tree call. If the gobbler answers, sit tight and listen for him to fly down.

If the gobbler is sounding off and you can hear hens roosted nearby, then sometimes it's good to go ahead and get your name in the hat. If you know for a fact that hens are going to fly down around the gobbler, then you may want to be the first hen to hit the ground. If the gobbler has answered your first soft calls, try a more aggressive call like a fly-down cackle. There is a chance that the gobbler may at least fly down in your direction. It could even provoke him to fly down sooner.

We all know that the reason a gobbler sits on the roost gobbling at sunrise is to call the hens to him. In most instances the gobbler won't even fly down until he sees a hen walk in. In areas with heavy hunting pressure, this is almost always is the case. Whenever a gobbler stops gobbling on the roost and seems to disappear, many hunters feel they did something wrong. Thoughts creep into your mind like, maybe I called too much, didn't call enough, moved in too close, set up too far away, or the always popular, the gobbler was call shy. It's possible that any of the above could have spoiled the hunt, but most often it was just hens. Most of us know that once a gobbler has spotted a hen from his roost, he will usually fly down and start his routine. He doesn't always continue to gobble at calls, be they yours or those of real hens.

Once this silence falls over the woods, many hunters feel defeated. More than likely, the gobbler is standing in the middle of his hens in full strut.

The law of averages and experienced turkey hunters will tell you that the classic "call him off the roost hunt" seldom happens. In most cases, the gobbler will fly down to his hens, and it's then the real hunt begins.

Beards and Spurs, Arrows and Nerves

I pulled the 65 pound bow to full draw and steadied my twenty-yard pin on the turkey's wing area. I knew an accurate shot in this spot would down any gobbler quickly. Just as my fingers were releasing the string, I heard a voice from behind:

"You big dummy, you can't kill a turkey with a bow."

The brand new shaft flew high over the gobbler's back and slammed into my neighbor's redwood fence. My setup was blown. Two of my hunting buddies had walked into my backyard when they spied my new life-size strutting gobbler archery target. As I tugged to retrieve the arrow from the fence, I listened to other rude comments about turkey hunting with a bow. My so-called buddies were really dishing it out.

"Hey Cuz, we'll go down to the Winn-Dixie and get 'em to hold you a butterball. Or better yet, we'll buy one of farmer Jim's turkeys and let it out. You might could get drawn on one of them barnyard turkeys. Ha Ha Ha."

Their laughter was deafening.

That was more than 10 years ago and to my buddies' surprise, and mine, I did manage to kill a turkey with my bow. It was a jake and it took almost three weeks of the season to get it done. Before releasing the arrow at that jake, I experienced some of the most nerve racking, tense and exhausting hunts I have ever been on. It seemed that time after time I would get into tight situations with turkeys and either not get drawn or not get the shot once I reached full draw. A real challenge? You bet.

Since that jake that became known to my hunting buddies as the "miracle bird," I have spent time in the woods with some of the best turkey hunters in the nation. Like me, most of them have taken a gobbler or two with archery gear, but few take their bows into the field each time they go turkey hunting. The level of the challenge is high and the difficulties are too numerous to mention while the chances for success are slim.

To walk into the woods, call up and take a turkey with a bow has to be one of the greatest and most difficult hunts in this country. To do so successfully takes a truly deep-seated dedication to practice, ethics and patience. There are few sportsmen who take on this challenge with the proper determination needed to be successful, considering the requirement of hours and hours of practice, the necessity of knowing when to pass the shot, and the dedicated patience it takes to wait for that perfect time to draw and release. Anyone who consistently kills turkeys with archery gear has taken their bowhunting and turkey hunting skills to an extremely advanced level.

The people who are successful at taking turkeys with a bow have some definite ideas about what tactics are needed. Recently I had the opportunity to visit with Jim Jordan of Tucson, Arizona. Jim is vice president of sales for PSE (Precision Shooting Equipment). While sitting in Jim's office, I could not help noticing some of the framed photos on the wall. Among the many happy hunter shots were several containing gobblers. I asked Jim if he had taken all of these gobblers with a bow, and he had.

Once the business side of our meeting was done, I began asking questions about his methods for bowhunting turkeys.

Like most truly successful hunters, Jim was very opinionated about his tactics. With the exception of his favorite honey holes, he was very free with his information and good solid advice on the sport.

After I had written down all of Jim's tips, I realized we had spent much more time talking turkeys and bowhunting than business. I also realized this guy knew what he was talking about. Here are Jim's 10 tips on taking turkeys with archery gear:

1. Make an effort to shorten the draw length on your bow. Jim uses a draw length a full inch shorter than normal on his turkey-hunting bow. The reason for this, he says, is all the awkward positions you can end up in while drawing on a turkey: Sitting flat on your butt, kneeling, on one knee, etc. The shorter draw length makes it easier to come to full draw in any position.

2. Set your draw weight for turkey hunting, get in all the above-mentioned positions and draw your bow slowly five times. Sit flat on your butt, stretch high on your knees and see if you can com-

fortably draw and hold your bow for extended periods of time under these conditions. If you can, your draw weight is fine.

3. Choose the best possible broadhead for the job. Through trial and error, Jim is now a firm believer in the mechanical type broadheads for turkeys. He prefers heads that open on impact like the Spitfire or the Vortex, and the bigger the better. Jim feels the large cutting width of these heads makes them the only choice for successfully taking turkeys. He said the last four gobblers he has taken with a bow all fell quickly to one of these mechanical heads.

4. Match your hunting style to the task at hand. Jim likes to stay very mobile, ready to move at any moment. He says one of the best tools he has for chasing gobblers is a turkey vest. Like most good turkey hunters, Jim carries a wide variety of calls. He says all the calls, combined with the extra gear you need for bowhunting, make a vest a must. Jim likes the Mossy Oak Longbeard vest, which features several large pockets, a detachable cushion and lightweight construction.

5. Know your territory before the hunt begins. Jim's success with turkeys goes back to good solid knowledge of where the turkeys are. He says you should make sure you cover enough ground when looking for a turkey hunting spot. Ask around and find the best possible place with the least amount of hunting pressure. Jim realizes that turkeys that are hunted hard are hard to hunt.

6. Make a concentrated effort toward becoming invisible. Full and total camouflage is a must. Jim says you can't be too careful when trying to fool turkeys' eyes. PSE offers dozens of their bows and accessories in Mossy Oak camouflage. Jim uses Mossy Oak camouflage while turkey hunting and likes to mix and match his upper and lower patterns to help break up his outline. He also stresses the need to cover everything that might shine. The head-to-toe camo edict includes your equipment.

7. Practice the same way you plan to hunt. Once you have all your camo and equipment ready, practice in it. Jim says he spends at least two or three practice sessions in full hunting gear including headnet, gloves and vest. This is the time to find any hidden problems that might cost you a shot in the field.

8. Make sure you have dull drab colors on your vanes or feathers. Jim says many people will have total camouflage on their

clothing and equipment and still have bright fluorescent colors on their arrow vanes. He recommends dark greens, browns or blacks to keep from alerting turkeys.

9. Try teamwork. Jim says success comes best when he uses the buddy system. He compares it to elk hunting with archery gear. He believes with a caller behind him, the hunted turkey will be more focused on the calling and less likely to see him when he makes his draw. If you can team up when bowhunting and calling any critter, your chances are better.

10. Ask questions when knowledgeable people are available. Jim's last bit of advice is truly golden. He said some of his most valuable knowledge of turkey hunting has come from asking experts. If you get a chance to ask a noted turkey-hunting expert a question, do so. There is no such thing as a stupid question.

Jim's advice alone is more than enough to give anyone interested in bowhunting turkeys a jump-start. I did, however, have the chance to meet and hunt with another true expert on this topic who was willing to offer up some additional advice on bowhunting turkeys.

Bill Zearing, of Halifax, Pennsylvania, owns and operates the Cody Call Company. Bill is not only one of the best turkey hunters and callers in the nation, he is also one of his region's best tournament archers. He shoots in 3-D matches year round and is very dedicated to the sport of archery. I had the pleasure of hunting with Bill on several occasions and got to see him in action in the spring of 1995 while hunting in Texas.

Bill was helping guide in one of the Mossy Oak camps we have each spring in Texas. After all the Mossy Oak guests had bagged their gobblers, Bill and I slipped out for an afternoon hunt. He had been guiding all week and the Rio Grande gobblers were getting a bit tired of all the activity in the area. Through the course of the afternoon, I followed Bill and watched as he went about trying to locate a gobbler. His calling soon got a response from a nearby creek bed and two hours later he came to full draw. I watched as the arrow hit its intended mark. Bill was on the gobbler before the longbeard knew what happened. It was truly special to watch this man go about harvesting that gobbler with only one afternoon to hunt.

Bill's successful methods come from years of missed opportunities and blown set ups. He will be the first to tell you that he has spooked, missed and run off his share of gobblers when getting into bowhunting turkeys. He also has some definite ideas and what it takes to bring home the bird when using the stick and string. Some of Bill's tips sound much like Jim's ideas on the subject. Both men have learned the hard way that practice, patience and dedication are keys to being successful.

1. Reduce your bow's draw weight to give yourself an edge. Bill uses the same rig for turkeys that he does for whitetails. He reduces the draw weight by about ten pounds so he can hold the bow at full draw for long periods of time when necessary.

2. Find a broadhead that works for you. Bill has used all types of broadheads for turkeys.

He likes the mechanical type heads, but he also likes the Muzzy head combined with a Muzzy Grasshopper to help slow the arrow's penetration. The Muzzy and Grasshopper was the combination he was using when I hunted with him in Texas.

3. Make sure you're comfortable in your hunting gear. Bill is also a big believer in practicing in the same clothes, vest, and gear that you'll be hunting in. He says being comfortable and confident is a huge part of being accurate with shot placement.

4. Remain mobile to make the most of every situation. According to Bill, many people hunting turkeys with bows use large, portable blinds. He prefers to stay lightweight and very mobile. Bill says that using Mossy Oak camouflage head to toe and utilizing whatever natural cover is available works for him. He does stress the need to make sure you are totally camouflaged, including your gear.

5. Take advantage of what a decoy can do for you. Bill says one of the best tools for anyone trying to bag turkeys with a bow is a decoy. The new lightweight folding decoys weigh less than a single shotgun shell and can be carried in your pocket. Bill feels using a decoy will often make a gobbler strut more once he is in range. A strutting gobbler can be a better target when he is facing away from you.

6. Build a routine that helps you control your nerves while you take care of business. Bill says the excitement level in turkey hunting with a bow is extremely high. Even with all the hunting

experience he has, he still gets excited and nervous during the hunt. To help himself remember all the little things a bowhunter must do, Bill has a small checklist he goes over constantly. It simply reads: come to full draw, look through the peep, don't torque the bow, don't jerk--relax.

7. Learn to judge distance. Bill says that if there is one thing he practices more than any other, it is judging distance. It makes no difference what animal you're hunting, if you are bowhunting, judging distance is the most critical factor. Bill says to keep himself sharp, he shoots in 3-D archery tournaments as often as possible. He also says that he uses objects such as trees, bushes, logs or rocks for estimation. He feels using the animal is not as accurate as a landmark. Bill says that as soon as you sit down or set up, begin picking your landmarks. He likes to start at 10 yards and work outward.

8. Practice patience, as it is the key to bowhunting turkeys ethically. The last bit of advice from Bill is also, according to him, his most important statement. Don't take a shot until you're sure it is the best and most lethal angle you have. Turkeys have a small kill zone and arrow placement is critical.

I have called in many gobblers that stayed in bow range for long periods of time and never offered me the shot I wanted. Patience is the key. One thing is certain: If you pass up the shot because you're not sure, you will know instantly you did the right thing.

Both of these bowhutners have become successful at a sport that may be the most challenging in the outdoors. To call in and bag a wild turkey with bow and arrow is an incredible feat. Over the past decade, I have seen many people who take a bow out into the spring woods and try to harvest a gobbler. There are those who talk about it and those who do it. The ones who talk about it a lot are probably not the ones to listen to. The ones who are truly good at it are most likely too busy practicing to talk very much.

The people I have met who consistently take gobblers with a bow are dedicated to their practice methods, hunting methods and most of all, their ability to make the right decision on when to shoot and when to pass.

The Rules

I often get asked by beginning turkey hunters what I consider to be the most important thing to learn about turkey hunting. I always tell them "The Rules."

Rule number one is find a copy of Tom Kelly's book, "The Tenth Legion" and read it cover to cover at least twice. If you do this, then you'll know the rules. If not, then it will take you a few dozen years to learn all the rules.

Tom Kelly is to turkey hunting what Mickey Mantle is to baseball. Sure, there was baseball before and after Mickey, but his time and name are of the golden age. He was all that was good about the game. Tom is of a golden age. He began turkey hunting when turkeys were few. He honed his skills because he had to. Along with tactics for hunting, he learned and wrote about the rules. Fair chase, manners, ethics, woodsmanship, love of the land, love of the sport and, most of all, love of the wild turkey. If you need to ask how can one love a creature and also kill it, then you'll never understand the rules.

To me, rules usually mean manners. I love golf and grew up playing the game. Long before I learned how to hit the ball long or straight, which is still a challenge, I learned the rules. My father and my uncle Bill taught me many of the rules while walking along with them. I must have walked and carried clubs a thousand miles before I started playing alone. When I finally started playing with other golfers, I knew when to hit and when to wait, when to mark my ball, when to let someone play through and so on. I learned the proper manners and ethics before I played with other people.

Today I see many young golfers who have beautiful swings, great equipment and a vast knowledge of the game, but still don't know the rules.

I would rather play with a person who can't break 100 and knows the subtle courtesies of the game, than play with a scratch player who cares little about the rules.

The same principals apply to turkey hunting. I would rather

hunt with the worst caller in the woods who knows the rules than sit alongside a world class caller with no class. If your sole goal in golf is to play below par, then you may miss some of what makes the game special. If your sole goal in turkey hunting is to kill the most or the biggest, then you'll surely miss what makes this sport so special, and you will most likely do a lot of your hunting alone.

When dealing with the rules, there are no gray areas. It's all black and white. It's either wrong or right. Some hunters use temporary ignorance to break the rules. For instance, a hunter hears a gobbler from his listening post and makes his way in that direction.

While moving closer, he spots a vehicle already parked in the area. In his heart, he knows that vehicle belongs to a hunter who is already headed to the gobbler. In his mind, the hunter begins thinking, maybe this vehicle belongs to someone marking timber, maybe it belongs to a jogger, and maybe it was stolen and dumped here. He talks himself into pressing on and pretty soon he walks up on the owner of the vehicle who is indeed a hunter and is already set up on the gobbler. He spooks the turkey and spends a few minutes apologizing and then moves on.

Temporary ignorance? More like rude behavior.

An absence of manners does not apply only to the young or newly learning.

I witnessed first hand a veteran turkey hunter over the age of 50 display one of the worst rule violations in history. I was working in a sporting goods store in my hometown of Natchez, Mississippi, and was greeted daily during the spring turkey season with hunters and hunters' tales. I was a member of a hunting club that held some good turkey populations and only two other turkey hunters. One of the other hunters was a 19-year-old kid. He was a nice young man and was just getting into turkey hunting.

One day he was in the sporting goods store with several other turkey hunters and shared with me information about a gobbling turkey that he could not call up. On several occasions, he had the gobbler roosted, and had had several close encounters with the bird, but had no luck closing the deal. The area in which this gobbler was living was one of the few spots I had not hunted. I suggested to the kid he talk with the other turkey hunter in our club.

As stated earlier, this gentleman was in his mid-50s and had killed many turkeys. He was very familiar with the gobbler's ground and would surely be agreeable to advising this kid on how to get in and slay this demon. I thought the veteran hunter might even offer to go along and show the kid first hand some new tactics that might help him close the deal. After the young hunter shared all his information with the seasoned veteran, he left the sporting goods store with a couple of new ideas and headed for work. Three hours later, the gobbler in question was riding in the veteran turkey hunter's truck. The seasoned hunter had taken the hard earned information from this kid and used it to kill the gobbler on a mid-day set up.

I'm sure many seasoned hunters will smile when reading this. There is indeed a code of silence among many turkey hunters. After all, there are few things as valuable as a gobbling turkey and you never should tip your hand on a hot spot, but to take information from a kid who was asking for nothing more than advice and use it to kill the turkey, come on. I still say that this case was a clear rule violation and one that to this day still sticks in my mind as a pitiful example of how NOT to conduct yourself with young or learning hunters.

Over the years, I have witnessed many rule violations. Most come from long-time, experienced hunters who, for some reason or another, feel they must prove their hunting prowess each season. Take for example this person who was helping me put on a turkey hunt in Texas. I had several outdoor writers coming into camp. I also had five or six fellows in camp a day and a half early to scout, listen and generally get familiar with the areas they would be hunting. I had a pre-hunt meeting with everyone and assigned each guide an area. I spent several minutes going over the rules and made each point very clear. The last rule was issued twice so there would be no confusion. It was simple. Each guide could kill a gobbler only after their hunter had bagged their turkey. This was just to make sure that no hunting would take place before the guests arrived. If there were any two-year-old suicidal gobblers hanging around, I wanted to make sure they were still around when the outdoor writers began their hunt.

The first evening of scouting was typical springtime in south Texas. Gobbling started around 6 p.m. and increased until roost time. I was watching turkeys through binoculars near a windmill at around 7:30 p.m. when I heard a shotgun blast in the distance. I knew it was one of the guides and had a good idea of which one it was.

I said nothing that night while we ate and discussed what we had heard. Later that night, I overheard the guide in question bragging about taking his gobbler before all the guests got in camp and screwed up the hunting. I know for a fact that this guy had killed many gobblers. He had hunted all over the country and taken at least one of each species. Why he had to hurry and kill one more turkey I'll never know. I never said anything to him.

Another example of not knowing the rules happens to some people when, in their hurry to prove their hunting prowess, they loose respect for the wild turkey. For example, I was in a hunting camp one April along with several outdoor writers, some well-known turkey hunting personalities and some regular guys serving as land guides. Toward the end of the hunt, all of the invited guests and writers had taken their turkeys and were just sitting around camp for a last evening fish fry. That last afternoon, some of the hunting personalities and guides went out for an afternoon hunt on their own. This hunt soon turned into a competition to show the high-powered writers who the best hunter-slash-callers really were.

On returning to camp at sunset, a few of the famous personalities, as well as a few of the local guides, had turkeys. The local guides went about the task of preparing their turkeys for the freezer and or taxidermist while several of the well-known hunters continued to talk for hours about their skill and calling techniques and left their turkeys sitting in the warm night air unattended. We eventually tended to the gobblers and made sure none of the meat spoiled.

I hope I never get caught up in anything so much that I forget how wonderful an animal the wild turkey is and what a grand privilege it is to hunt these creatures each spring.

Breaking the rules happens in any sport. It happens wherever people are and there are rules to follow. It's clear to me that there are some people who will always think the rules don't apply to them. They have never understood and most likely never will. Learning how to live within the rules is taught to you early in life. You learn by example. Most hunters had a person in their lives who took time early on to teach them about the outdoors.

Hunting and fishing is a great time to show your children, or anyone else for that matter, how to follow rules. Respect for the game and fellow hunters is something that is taught early on. For one reason or another, some people get it, and some don't. For many people, the all-important dead animal in hand is how they feel judgment is passed on one's status with hunting peers. For me, the overall status of a hunter's skill is measured in many other ways. Sure, the hunts that end with a successful shot are special and are indeed a part of the sport. Anyone who devotes time to learning the game and secures a good place to hunt can achieve this goal. This level is often enough for many, but to me, the hunter who takes his or her knowledge and love of the sport and shares it with other people, especially kids and new hunters, is truly someone special, --and believe me, they know the rules.

"Many" years ago, 40 pounds lighter and with much darker hair, I had to work harder to hide with the old military camo. But, back then, there was less of me to hide.

When Mossy Oak camo first hit the market Toxey's ads declared, "it will change the way you hunt." It certainly changed the way I hunt.

Yelp Marks

When I was a kid, every time my Mom made homemade tea cakes, she would set aside some of the raw cookie dough just for me. This was then chilled, hidden in the fridge and saved for some special occasion. This was one of those rare treats that came along only once in a while. It was something you savored and thought about for days before actually caving in for the few moments of pleasure that came with devouring the dough raw.

Another rare and wonderful gift that comes along like Mom's homemade cookie dough is a loud-mouthed, long-bearded lonesome gobbler. He sounds off every morning and, better yet, lives in an area that holds few hens and in which no other turkey hunters are allowed. On a spring afternoon in 1984, I received both of these special gifts in a single day.

I had visited my parents' house on the way to the woods and, lo and behold, Mom had saved me some homemade cookie dough. Temptation got the better of me and I finished my treat while on the way to roost a gobbler for opening day. I didn't save even one bite for later. I wish I had been as smart with the gobbling turkey I was about to meet.

That afternoon I heard one gobbler at fly-up time. He was gobbling like crazy at some owls and I had permission to hunt that property all season.

I was scheduled to take a good buddy hunting on opening morning. This was to be his first turkey hunt, so the thought of having pinpointed a loud-mouthed gobbler had me excited to say the least. As luck would have it, my good buddy was unable to make the opening morning hunt. An unexpected change in his work schedule tied him up for most of the season. Since the loud-mouthed gobbler was in a remote area with no other hunters, I saved him.

For almost three weeks, I checked on this gobbler. I would go into his area at sunrise and he would gobble. I would go by in the evening and make him gobble with a simple owl hoot. He was always there and would always gobble.

With only 10 days remaining in the season, and my good buddy still unable to go on a hunt, the thought of that lovesick gobbler was more than I could stand. I called Bubba Bruce, another good friend and longtime turkey hunter, and invited him to take part in this gobbler's demise. I gave my friend the history of this turkey and told of how, on many occasions, I would stop and hoot and each time he would gobble. It was going to be a storybook hunt and Bubba would owe me big time for sharing this event with him.

The next morning, the weather conditions were perfect. My face was a bit sore from sleeping with a wide grin. To say I was confident would be an understatement. I picked Bubba up well before daylight and stopped at all the local coffee spots to make sure the other turkey hunters saw us and heard the statements I was making, guaranteeing a gobbler by 6:30 a.m., bold talk this late in the season.

Bubba and I made our way through the woods and stopped a few hundred yards of the ridge where Old Faithful lived. I was just about to owl hoot when I heard Bubba whisper, "yelp mark." I turned to see Bubba kneeling down looking at a fresh boot track.

"What did you say?"

He replied again, "A yelp mark."

I asked Bubba to define a yelp mark.

"Fresh sign left by another turkey hunter."

He went on to say that in his estimation, this was indeed the boot track of a turkey hunter. He also added that this hunter might have already killed the turkey that I had been saving all season. I wrote Bubba's comments off to his lack of sleep since early March. I decided to let him hear my gobbler and did my best imitation of a barred owl. No response.

I owled again. No response. We walked closer to the gobbler's favorite ridge and finally stopped in the same area where I had heard the gobbler only two mornings earlier. I was reaching in my vest for a slate call when I heard Bubba once again.

"Bad yelp mark."

I looked, and there by a large white oak tree was a cleaned out place on the ground and a spent shotgun shell. I picked up the shell and detected the faint smell of gunpowder. Bubba just shook his head and walked back toward the truck.

"I hate yelp marks," he said as he walked down the ridge.

Old Faithful did not gobble that morning. Looking back, I realize that I should have hunted that turkey sooner. With more turkey hunters in the woods today than ever, the chances of a loud - mouthed gobbler going un-hunted in any area is slim.

Learning how to share the woods with other hunters is something that many of us just learn to deal with. I grew up hunting national forest land and looking back, I believe it made me a better hunter. I learned how to look for signs of other hunters as well as hide my own. It was just a matter of trying to maximize your chances on public ground. On many occasions, I had hunts ruined by people walking in on my set up, especially turkey hunting set ups. I eventually learned to avoid areas that other hunters would frequent and would make myself walk that extra mile to get into quieter woods.

Today I hunt mainly on private land, but yelp marks are just about as frequent. The signs of other turkey hunters can tell you a lot about what you're faced with in your hunting area. If you see ATV tracks all through the woods, then you know you're dealing with a guy who is most likely not a serious turkey hunter. If he rides to cover most of the area he hunts, then he is not a real threat to most of the turkey population. That doesn't mean there's anything wrong with using ATVs to hunt. I have one myself and use it a lot. I just don't use it to slip around and locate turkeys that much.

The casual turkey hunter tends to approach turkey hunting the same as deer hunting. He will more than likely hang out with other turkey hunters prior to the season, then hunt the opening weekend and maybe once or twice more. This guy will quickly tire of the 4 a.m. routine, bugs and approaching warm temperatures. He will not be much competition after the first week. All in all, ATV tracks are not that bad of a yelp mark. They tend to look like there have been lots of heavy traffic but also disappear early in the season.

This next turkey hunter is a bit more competition. He leaves small yelp marks but they may be around for the whole season. If you see the same boot prints in lots of hard-to-reach spots that require a good deal of effort to reach, then you can bet this guy is serious and will not hesitate to cover lots of ground silently to locate turkeys. The good news here is this person won't spook many turkeys. He will slip in and out and probably respect your space if he hears you calling or sees your vehicle. The best way to handle the hard-core turkey hunter who is sharing your woods is to try and be his buddy. Try to strike up a conversation and see if you can work out a system of splitting the territory on a daily basis.

He may become a hunting friend. If not, try and at least find out what type of calls he uses most when hunting and locating. Then you can avoid those calls that you know turkeys are hearing when he is in the area.

If he prefers a box call for locating, avoid it. If he uses a mouth call most of the time, then you try a slate or tube call. Also try and find out when this guy hunts the most. If he does all his hunting in the morning, then try hunting mid-morning or after-noon if it's legal in your state. If he gets weekends off, try to hunt before work during the week.

Another type of hunter who is common in any turkey woods is the sitter. He doesn't leave many yelp marks but his marks are deep. He will find a likely place for turkeys, most often a field, and stake his claim. He will build a blind out of limbs and brush and some camouflage material. He will sit in this area day after day and will yelp softly once in a while and cluck two or three times in an hour.

Once I have found the sitter's yelp marks, I will avoid his area all together. He is generally an older person, most likely retired and very patient. He will not wander around calling and will not under any circumstances spook turkeys. He will take several people (one at a time) on a hunt during the course of the season, and will most like-ly show them some turkeys. He hunts deer the same way and usu-ally is successful taking a buck or two each season. Another thing about this guy, he will probably kill the biggest gobbler in the area and tell everyone that you call too much and too loud.

The last type of hunter who makes his share of yelp marks is a rare breed. He is the guy who has reached another level in turkey hunting skill. This guy can call like the sweetest hen you ever heard. He can cover more ground in one day than you would believe. He can use every type of turkey call ever made, including wing bones and tube calls. When trying to locate gobblers, he can generate enough volume with a box, slate, tube or mouth call to shake leaves from the trees. When he needs to bring a hung-up gobbler in those last 50 yards, he can reproduce soft hen sounds so real you would think she is purring right beside you. He can sweet-talk any landowner into letting him hunt their property. He can persuade the mailman, the bus driver, and numerous delivery men into spilling their best keep secrets about where turkeys are.

This guy is not only skilled at all aspects of turkey hunting; he has the mental attitude of Vince Lombardi. He knows in his mind that if there is a gobbler in hearing range of him, he can make him gobble or at least locate him and then successfully hunt him. He does not give up easily and is confident of his ability to locate even seasoned old gobblers that gobble very little. The tougher the challenge, the more he gets into the hunt. This guy will leave yelp marks on purpose. If he is sharing land with another seasoned turkey hunter, then much of the game will be played with another person as well as turkeys.

He will leave boot prints where he wants you to think he is hunting. He will leave no marks where he is on turkeys. He will drop hints that will mislead another hunter and would not divulge the location of a gobbler if he were being tortured. Trying to read this guy's yelp marks is a waste of time. He has made a life out of turkey hunting. It is who he is and what he is known for. If you're sharing your turkey woods with one of these guys, my suggestion is to change your hunting area or at least find property that he cannot hunt.

For another perspective on dealing with yelp marks, I talked with 33-year-old Bob Walker of Livingston, Alabama. Bob has dozens of professional turkey calling titles including the Alabama State Championship. Bob is a full-time guide at Bent Creek Lodge and takes clients hunting every day during the long Alabama season. Even though Bent Creek lodge has more than 30,000 acres for hunting, Bob switches areas from time to time. When going into another area that has been hunted, he will always find out what guide was most recently hunting that spot. Since all the guides are familiar with their calling techniques and preferred calls, Bob will make sure he uses different calls and less of them.

He explains, "As the season wears on, turkeys get more aware of being hunted. Less calling and more walking is usually what I end up doing. Most turkeys are used to getting called to from a road or within the same area. Most people come into an area on a road and owl. If they hear a gobbler, they go straight to him. If I get on a gobbler that I know has been called to some, I prefer to flank him and set up to one side or even behind him. I then will usually call very little, maybe scratch in the leaves and be patient."

Bob also has some additional sound advice when hunting any area that has other turkey hunters around.

"Safety is always my first concern when hunting in an area with other hunters," he says. "I always assume that any turkey sound is another hunter. Today callers are so good that often times you cannot tell the difference between hunters and the real thing. I approach any turkey sound with caution and always hunt defensively. For me at least, dealing with other hunters has become less of a negative issue over the years. I enjoy taking new hunters. I take pleasure in hunting with seasoned veterans of the sport and always enjoy meeting new people.

"I have hunted with some of the greatest turkey hunters in the nation and learned something different from all of them. I have been told I call too much. I have been told I call too loud. I have been told I don't call enough. I have even been told that I move too much and sit in one place too long. There is no other sport that will spring as many good-natured arguments and hard-headed advice as turkey hunting."

One common thread that runs through all of us who chase turkeys in the spring: we all leave a few yelp marks.